M000200661

WAKING UP IN THE MIDDLE OF NOWHERE

Allison Johnson

EAGLE ROCK PUBLISHERS
www.eaglerockbooks.com

Waking Up in the Middle of Nowhere will rock your world! Told with insight and sensitivity, Allison's story alternately stuns and inspires. Ultimately, it will equip you to bridge the gap for others who are caught between two poles."
Jerome Daley, ACC, DPM, Leadership Coach, author

There is a moment that comes in a person's life when expectation meets reality. The size of the gulf between these extremes often determines the level of disappointment we face in life. For Allison Johnson, that chasm seemed like the Grand Canyon when she was faced with the reality that her husband, Grant, was suffering with bipolar disorder. Her book, *Waking Up in the Middle of Nowhere*, is a gripping memoir of their journey from the darkness of untreated disease to the light of hope through a combination of love and forgiveness, balanced with spiritual guidance and medical intervention. It is a story of coming to peace with a God who does not always deliver us from our pain and suffering, but who always loves us and strengthens us to help us endure. It is the tale of a family who chose love over selfishness and hope over fear. For the person who loves someone with bipolar disorder, this memoir will be a friend in the storm, helping you to hold on until the sun shines through the clouds once again.
Craig Von Buseck, Director of Ministries, Christian Broadcasting Network, CBN.com

Waking Up in the Middle of Nowhere gives the reader a unique perspective into the life of one whose spouse is bipolar. I have read many excellent books on the subject of bipolar disorder, but never one from the perspective of the patient's spouse. This book is a real help to the person whose mate struggles with this disorder. But the author also gives the one suffering from bipolar disorder a wealth of insight into how their illness is affecting the entire family. If you and a loved one are dealing with this disorder, or you know a family who is, *Waking Up in the Middle of Nowhere* is a must read.
Rick Surley, M.A. Marriage and Family Therapist

Allison's story of despair transformed into victory is at once captivating, gut-wrenching, and full of hope. From the first chapter, you are welcomed into a world that all too many people know, and too few are willing or able to share with others. But with Allison and Grant, the door is courageously flung open so that others who live in the same kind of world can find real hope for healing and restoration. Thanks Allison, for inviting us in!
Roger Erdvig, M.Ed. President, Center for the Advancement of Christian Coaching

By telling her story with honesty and candor, Allison Johnson offers encouragement and hope to those in bipolar marriages who feel alone and afraid. *Waking Up in the Middle of Nowhere* is a gift to anyone needing to know that someone else has been there and understands the challenges, heartaches, and triumphs unique to a bipolar marriage.
Joanne Heim, author of *Misplacing God: And Finding Him Again* **and** *Living Simply: Choosing Less in a World of More*

Allison Johnson has penned a graceful, gracious, gripping memoir of a marriage brought back from the brink. She offers much needed insight to the perplexing illness of bi-polar disorder; how to survive when a loved one is mentally ill; and how to preserve love, faith, and sanity when it seems your world is falling apart. Whether or not you have grappled with mental illness or marital strife, *Waking Up in the Middle of Nowhere* will leave you breathless and restore your hope in the God for whom nothing is impossible.
Sharon L. Fawcett, author of *Hope for Wholeness: The Spiritual Path to Freedom from Depression*

WAKING UP IN THE MIDDLE OF NOWHERE
Copyright ©2010 by Allison Johnson
Published by Eagle Rock Christian Publishers
Eugene, Oregon 97404
www.eaglerockbooks.com

ISBN 978-1-60914-002-1

The Holy Bible, New International Version (NIV) © 1973, 1984 by International Bible Society, used by permission of Zondervan Publishing House.

Disclaimer:
We are not experts. We are not doctors or scholars when it comes to marriage and mental illness, specifically bipolar. And we would never assume that what works for us, will work for everybody else. We are, however, battle weary survivors hoping to impart to you some of the practical aspects of how we persevered through our own trip through hell on earth.
   * Some names have been changed.

ALL RIGHTS RESERVED. No part of this publication may be reproduced, stored in a retrieval system, or transmitted in any form or by any means - electronic, mechanical, digital photocopy, recording, or any other - except for brief quotations in printed reviews, without the prior permission of the publisher.

Published in the United States of America.

ACKNOWLEDGEMENTS

To my parents, thank you for loving me and Grant without condition, and for the amazing grace and self-less love you gave. These gifts helped to carry us through our darkest hour.

To Grant's parents, whose unconditional love helped him through one of his darkest periods.

To my sisters and brother, I would not be the same without you by my side. You are my best friends and I love you.

To my sweet network of friends, Jaime, Carla, Carrie, Martha, Veronica, Stephanie, Patti and Samantha, your friendship is a gift I will always treasure. Thank you for loving me and my family.

To Carrie and Martha for being there from the beginning, words cannot express what the two of you did for me on that day, you Rock!

To Rick, Jerome and Brenda, thank you for being like Jesus to me.

To my agent Bill Jensen, for believing in me and for making our book a reality. Here's to the Bohemians.

To Zachary and Kayla, I'm proud of you and so glad you're mine. Love you.

To Grant,

You are that man. You are the man that fills my dreams.
You are the man I long for, the man that makes my heart
sing.
You are the one; I know you are the one.
It is you…

CONTENTS

CHAPTER ONE

Freefalling

What I expect to be real isn't. I try to cling to the tattered edges of reality, desperately grasping for anything that might make things right again. I flail around clutching at the air, clawing for anything to help me. Some small branch, a twig, anything...I can't see but I know I'm freefalling into a dark black pit where the fire burns all around.

Tuesday, August 16, 2005
6:25am [San Antonio, TX]

"Good bye," Grant whispered into my ear as I struggled to wake myself from a sound sleep. He kissed me lightly on my lips as my eyes opened. I quickly wrapped my arms around his neck whispering, "I love you. Have a good trip." He nodded, and I watched as he quietly left our bedroom. He was heading for Dallas for the next twenty-four hours. I couldn't help but wonder if it wasn't a good thing. I flopped back down on the pillows for a moment, glancing at the clock, it was 6:25. I still had five minutes before the kids would be up for their second day of second grade. I tried to close my eyes and rest, but a familiar tide of melancholy washed over my heart as I began mulling over the previous night's argument.

I didn't understand what was happening to us; it seemed like all we did was fight lately. There was nothing I knew to say that made anything better; in fact, whatever I tried just made things worse. It was always the same old thing: I didn't appreciate him, he was just a meal ticket, and I was never going to understand how hard he worked to make me happy. I sighed, and rolled over…staring out the window for a moment before I decided to shake it off and hop out of bed.

We had always worked things out before; there was no reason for me to think we wouldn't work this one out now. I promised myself I would pray, seek God's guidance, and continue to ask Him to show me where I was wrong. I knew it was important to Grant to respect and honor him, and definitely I loved him. It just felt so hard. I wanted to show him how much I appreciated all he did, but I didn't know how. Last night's argument had been a bad one and I was scared.

As I wandered out to start the coffee in the kitchen I could hear Zach and Kayla moving about in their rooms. They were still excited about starting second grade. They were such great kids, and I knew they would be running down here any second, bursting with excitement to hurry up and get out the door. If I could stall them for a few minutes, I might be able to quickly check my email before we ate breakfast. I met both of them at the top of the stairs and instructed them to go make their beds and put their dirty clothes away. "Mommy is going to check her email. Why don't you guys come to the game room when you're finished, and then we'll go downstairs together." They groaned, but raced each other back to their rooms to see who could make their bed the fastest. I chuckled as I sat down at my computer; man, I didn't want them to grow up.

6:43am

I wiggled the mouse, and the screen saver popped up. As I rolled the cursor to my outlook express icon, I noticed several minimized icons at the bottom of the page. Huh, I wonder what happened here. Maybe one of the kids had been playing on the computer last night and I didn't notice it. Oh well, that's easy enough: I'll just close these out before I open my email. I could hear the kids chattering to each other; it would only be a moment before they came racing in. I better hurry up.

With a click of my mouse the first icon expanded on my screen. I was expecting Dora the Explorer or Disney Channel, but I caught my breath in surprise and horror, my brain struggling to comprehend what I was looking at. The website was filled with tombstones and grave markers, and at the very front of the page was a gray, sculpted tombstone of beautifully hewn marble, inscribed, Grant Johnson, July 17, 1970- August 2005. My heart pounded in my ears, and my stomach began to churn.

Numbly, now, I clicked the next icon. A coffin. A beautifully crafted oak-colored coffin with cream satin lining was featured on the page. *What kind of cruel joke is this?* I couldn't fathom what I was seeing; this couldn't be real. My hands were shaking as I expanded the final icon. Exploding onto my screen were the Air Force Academy guidelines to be buried on Academy grounds. Grant's name was filled in as the deceased.

I fought the urge to vomit as stomach bile filled the back of my throat. Blinded by tears, I choked back the sobs that were clutching at my throat. I could hear the voices of my children in their rooms down the hall, sunlight was drifting in through the window blinds, coffee was in my mug, and I was staring at a computer screen decorated with cryptic messages of my husband's death. None of it made sense to me, none of it at all. I quickly minimized the icons and tried to breathe again. Fire flickered around the edges of my vision, and my head was filled with the sounds of my own voice screaming, "Oh Dear God, Oh Dear God!"

Something switched inside of me as I jumped out of the chair: *I must get my kids to school. I cannot fall apart right now. I have to get through the next thirty minutes.* A saying from my Healing Hearts class drifted into my consciousness, "When you don't know what to do, do normal things." I said it again, and I kept repeating it to myself in my head while I made Zach and Kayla's breakfast. *Do normal things.*

I spread peanut butter on bread, smeared jelly on the other, slapping them together to make a sandwich. *Normal things.* I fed the dog. I brushed Kayla's hair. I made myself another cup of coffee. *Normal things.* I helped them pack their backpacks, gave a quick instruction on shoelace tying for Zach, and tried to suppress the hysterical voice inside. "Finish your breakfast, Kayla. Brush your teeth, Zach," a forced smile on my face. Meanwhile, I made a quick call to my friend Martha, "Do you think you could stop by my house on your way to work, I've got something I need to show you?"

When I hung up, I continued with normal. It was automatic now. I smiled at my neighbors, made chitchat with one of the mothers at the school gate. *Just keep doing normal.* I even took Yukon for a walk, grabbed a shower, and decided that today was definitely a no-makeup kind of day. But despite my best attempts at normalcy, my entire body was quaking, my head pounding, and icy tentacles of fear were gripping my heart so tightly that I knew something was terribly, terribly wrong. I had little idea of what to do…and no idea what was coming next.

8:30am

I ran to the front door, and as much as I wanted to throw myself into Martha's arms, I contained myself and invited her into the kitchen. I sat down politely, "Would you like a drink? Coffee? Tea? Water?" She shook her head no, inviting me to begin.

"I can't even begin to tell you how glad I am that you're here," I said across the table. "It has been a very difficult couple of days, and I have no idea what's really going on."

Martha's face eased into a quiet smile and she said, "Allison, why don't you tell me, and we will take it one step at a time." I sat back in my chair, wondering if speaking these horrible things out loud would make them true. And then, the words found their way through the cracks in my façade and began to trickle out. Then they began to pour.

I told her about the awful fights, how Grant kept telling me how much he hates being married to me. How selfish I am and how unhappy he is. The words came rapidly now as I found courage in speaking the truth and threw down my makeshift walls of denial. I showed her the picture of the little blonde girl crying beside a tombstone for Santa Claus. And I described for her, in his words, how the little girl is me, and I am crying because my Santa Claus is gone.

I felt lost now, in a raging torrent determined to throw me outside the realm of my sanity. But there was more. I told her about the scripture verses he had written on our bathroom mirror and kitchen counter...about death, meaningless living and leeches that are never satisfied. I told her about the motorcycle he'd bought and his plan to go pick it up in Atlanta and how I will never understand him even though I've tried. I told her about the morbid photographs on my computer and how he's gone to Dallas for business and how I'm afraid he's not coming back.

9:15am

My head hurt as I looked at Martha across the table, waiting for her to say something. *I am floating on the backs of the words I have spoken. They are real now, and I grip them tightly.* "Allison, I think we should go and

look at the computer, and you can show me the pages you were talking about." I nodded my head and we moved noiselessly upstairs to the computer.

"Martha, why don't you go ahead and open them, and I'll sit here." She agreed and one by one she clicked each icon open, expanding the photos of coffins, tombstones, and burial instructions across the computer screen. *I wonder what she's thinking.*

She turned to me with sober eyes. And I know even before she says it. "Allison, I think we have a very serious problem." I stared blankly at her for a moment before I replied, "Yeah, I thought so."

The screams are mine, but I don't recognize their sound. I'm plummeting, into darkness. The putrid scent of death wraps itself around me. My skin burns as the sulfuric claws of hell wrench my heart from my body, squeezing until I gasp for breath. My mind is calling, "Won't someone help me! PLEASE!" But I can't make the words; no one will hear me above the howling. I'm in hell, and my words are gone.

9:20am

"Allison, I'm going to make some calls. If you can, you need to print those pages from the computer." Martha stared at the crumpled heap of my body as I lay on the game room floor. "Allison, I know this is hard. You're going to get through this." I nodded my head as she walked out of the room. *Get through this? How?* I pulled myself off the floor and dumbly activated the printer just as she asked.

Printed papers in hand, I wandered down the stairs

and heard her on the phone. As I rounded the last few steps, she saw me and moved out the front door. I watched her close the door behind her and figured she was telling someone that I'd completely lost it and that my husband had too. In fact, it wouldn't have surprised me at all if someone had shown up at my front door with a straitjacket and carted me off to the insane asylum. *That would have been far better than being in hell,* I thought grimly.

Standing in the sunlight by the front door, I watched Martha gesture wildly with her hands to someone on the phone. It was going to be a pretty day; I could feel the warmth of the sun on the front window. Waves of guilt mixed with fear washed over me now. I felt bad for involving Martha in this fiasco. I felt guilty for needing help. I felt weak for not knowing what to do. I hated what was happening, and I was terrified. Martha's words sifted through the door, "I don't know what to do. I wasn't trained for this. But she's holding up okay." *Hah, that's funny.*

Out of the corner of my eye I saw Grant's desk inviting me to keep it company for a while so I disappeared into his giant chair. I sank into the folds of leather willing myself to invisibility. With eyes closed, I imagined the four of us the way we were when we were happy. I thought of the way the kids climbed all over him, and he pretended to collapse under their weight, his laughter mixed in with theirs. His smile, and the way he said just the right thing and made me grin even when I didn't want to. I could feel the warmth of his big fingers, caressing mine the way they did when we sat together and just enjoyed being close. *Jesus, could you come back right now? Please could you rescue me from this?*

I ran my hands over the smooth lines of the wood desk. His office smelled like a mixture of printer ink, cherry hardwoods, and rich cigar tobacco. Papers were strewn across the top of his desk, and mountains of books were piled next to the bookshelf. In spite of myself, I almost laughed out loud. He definitely had his own way of organizing his stuff. I closed my eyes again and saw him sitting there on the phone handling an important call. I saw him doodling on his notepad or chewing on an unlit cigar while processing some important deal. I would stand in the doorway sometimes, just to hear the smooth inflection of his voice as he beckoned someone into a new way of thinking. He was good at that, changing people's minds.

Jolted out of my reverie my eyes flew open. There had to be something I was missing. Something, somewhere that I could grab hold of to make sense of this mess. I opened drawers, driven by an anxious hunger to immerse myself in his stuff. I was possessed by a new and strange curiosity to understand this man whom I had loved for 12 years. I was desperate to find something about him I might recognize. I dug through photos of Zach and Kayla, chocolate Reisen candy, pipe tobacco, pens, paper, and a list of goals with checkmarks next to the goals accomplished.

I thought if I could find clues that gave a direction to follow, perhaps that would call him home. I opened the last drawer and there sitting on the top of the stack was an envelope. My eyes burned with fire as I picked it up. With shaking hands I turned it over and then turned it over again. My name and address were on the front, it was stamped and the return address was Grant Johnson. What I hadn't counted on in my quest for clues was an answer, and I held it in my hand.

7:50am [Yakima, WA]
9:50am [San Antonio, TX]

"Hello?" My dad's groggy voice momentarily soothed my frayed nerves, and my heart found comfort. *Surely Dad would know what to do.* I wished I could hang up without saying the awful truth, but I desperately needed him. I needed someone to tell me that everything was going to be all right. I needed someone to be strong, wise, and decisive. Of all the qualities my dad possessed, my favorite was his ability to act without hesitation. He knew what to do and when to do it. "Allison, is that you?"

I took a deep breath, and steadied my quivering voice. "Yes, Dad it's me. Sorry to call so early, but I have an emergency. A life and death emergency, and it has to do with Grant."

As he struggled to sit upright in bed, the early morning sun poured through his window slats. "What? What did you say?" He was awake and alert, but he couldn't make sense of my words.

"Dad, I found several things this morning that make me believe Grant is going to commit suicide." I quickly gave him the bottom line: Grant was gone. I didn't know if he was coming back. And I needed help. "Dad, I need you!" My voice shook, and I started to cry. Through my sobs my tiny voice squeaked out, "Dad, I'm scared, can you come?" I heard him breathing on the other end, calculating what he'd been told. And then his voice came strongly over the line, "Honey, I'll be right there."

Relief washed over me as he asked a few more questions. I told him that Martha was with me and to call her from now on. I wasn't answering the phone anymore. She was handling everything.

7:55am [Yakima, WA]

My dad hung up the phone with me and in the same motion dialed my brother Frankie. He glanced at the clock and decided Frankie shouldn't be flying yet. Probably still unloading freight, he thought, if he's even at the airport yet.

Frankie answered on the third ring, "What's up, Dad."

My dad spoke to Frankie in his most serious voice. This was the no arguing voice, the voice that could make our neck hair stand up as kids and even still as adults. "Frankie, I need you home right away."

When my dad hung up the phone, his head fell into his outstretched hands. His throat closed like a dam, cutting off the sobs of fear that welled inside him. He wondered, what in the world is happening? He struggled to wrap his mind around what I had said to him on the phone as he threw things into a suitcase. Grants plans to kill himself would never make sense to him. He dialed my sister Holly and realized he had never felt so afraid. *Shirts, shorts, shaving kit*, he couldn't think. What else? Holly's voice crackled over the line. "Hello."

"Holly," my dad croaked, "I've got to get to San Antonio as soon as possible. Grant is on a suicide mission. Allison just called, and she needs our help. Can you get me and your mom on a flight as soon as possible?" Silence…

"Holly, are you there?"

"Yes. Um…Dad? How soon do you want to leave?" He could tell by the sound of her voice that she was stunned and like him was trying to come to grips with what he'd said.

"As soon as possible," he replied, "and book a separate flight for your mom; she's got to come in from Wenatchee. Oh, and Holly, I almost forgot, happy birthday." He snapped his phone shut, knowing there would be time for questions and answers later. Now with the plans set in place he felt a new sense of direction.

He strode into the bathroom running his hands through what little hair he had left. While he brushed his teeth he told himself over and over, *Get it together, man, get it together.* Throwing his toothbrush into his bag he wished desperately for my mom, Cathy. The thought of calling her comforted him as he tossed the final pieces of clothing into his suitcase.

Of all the things my dad had ever imagined for his family, the idea of losing one of his kids to suicide had never entered his mind…and Grant *was* like a son to him. He told me all the time how blessed he felt because he knew that I had such a great husband. In fact I enjoyed telling him of Grant's daily successes at work and all the ways he cared for me at home because I loved hearing the sound of pride in his voice. I knew that my dad just couldn't imagine life without Grant and like me would do whatever he could to save him.

The front door slammed and the sound of my brothers' footsteps echoed through the empty house. He appeared in the doorway of my parents' bedroom his face contorted with worry. He caught his breath and blurted out, "Dad, what in the world is going on?"

My dad stood up quickly smoothing the comforter on the bed and said, "Son, I'll tell you on the way, but right now you've got to get me to the airport as fast as you can and get me on a flight to Seattle."

They ran down the hall together with separate missions but were united by the burden of fear that consumed their hearts. Frankie whipped out his phone, called his friend at the airport, and immediately my dad had a seat on the next flight to Seattle. He was on his way to rescue me and to do whatever he could to help me save my husband.

8:00am [Seattle, WA]

"Ranne!" My sister Holly yelled from her kitchen as she hung up with our Dad.

"Ranne, I need you. Please come down!" She tried to calm the tremor in her voice as her two children stared at her with curiosity. Her husband Ranne tumbled down the stairs and flew into the kitchen saying with irritation, "What! Why are you yelling at me?"

Holly grabbed his arm and dragged him away from their kids, quickly briefing him on the crazy phone call she'd just had from our dad. And then she waited.

Ranne blinked at her for about a second and said, "Okay, how do you want to do this?"

She hugged him appreciatively and said, "You get on your cell phone. I'll get on the house phone, and let's call the same airline at the same time and see if we can't get something coordinated as close to the same landing time as possible." He looked sideways at her, and she immediately knew what he was thinking. Smiling back at him she said, "Yeah, I know, happy birthday to me."

8:15am [Wenatchee, WA]

Who could be calling this early? My Mom had gone to her friend Marsha's condo to relax and enjoy some quiet time...which included quiet time from family members. Irritated by the interruption to her morning, she was tempted to just let the phone ring. But after a few rings she decided to check the caller ID. Maybe I can call them back, she thought as my dad's number flashed across the screen. She groaned inwardly, set down her tea and flipped open her phone.

"Hi Frank," she greeted him coolly, wondering why he couldn't wait to talk with her until after her first cup of tea.

"Cathy, we have an emergency," he said choking

back tears. "Grant is on a suicide mission, and I'm on my way to the airport right now. Holly is working on getting us tickets out of Seattle today. You need to call her and tell her how soon you can get to Seattle. She'll have a flight for you."

Moms head spun as she tried to make sense of what he was saying. "What did you say? Did you say Grant is going to kill himself?"

"Yes. Allison called and we need to get to San Antonio right away." My dad paused, letting his words sink in. "I have to go now, but call Holly and I'll call you when I land. I'm getting on a flight now."

Okay, he's serious, she thought. This is not a nightmare, and yet her brain could not comprehend what he was saying.

"Frank, is she okay? Did she sound all right on the phone?" Mom asked him as tears ran down her cheeks. *Oh my sweet girl. What's happening? Oh God, please help us.*

"Yes," he replied, but he wasn't sure he really believed I was going to be alright. He continued consoling my Mom with words he tried to believe. "She's scared but she's not alone. She's got a friend with her who is handling her calls. I've got to get on my flight, now." And then he whispered, "Honey, I love you."

"I love you too," and she hung up her phone.

10:00am [San Antonio, TX]

The envelope burned in my hand. I felt my brain frantically trying to catch up with the rhythm of my racing heart. *It couldn't be!* Even with everything I had seen that morning, somewhere buried deep inside me had been a small flicker of hope. I kept imagining he was going to come strolling through the door shouting, "Surprise! It's just a joke!" But now...the burden of truth settled itself inside me and snuffed out that voice of denial.

I wilted in the chair as Martha walked back in the door. She was still on the phone. Taking one look at me, she saw the unopened letter in my hand and promptly whisked it away. I heard her say to someone, "Yes, it looks like we have a suicide note."

Oh my God! My heart, oh my love! Where have you gone? What have you done? My sweet love, please come home!

I dragged myself to the kitchen where I politely answered questions from the lady on the suicide hotline. Martha convinced me that we needed to find a place for Zach and Kayla to go after school. I called my friend Carrie. As soon as she answered, I handed the phone to Martha. *How can I explain this horrific situation?* I packed overnight bags for the kids and wondered what kind of home they would return to.

CHAPTER TWO

Love and Marriage, Right?

"...And your endurance inspired by hope in our Lord Jesus Christ." 1 Thessalonians 1:3

10:45am Tuesday

I closed the front door behind me, not bothering to lock it. What if he came home while we were gone? I couldn't remember if he had a key. I felt the August sun hot on my face as I turned to trudge across the grass to Martha's truck. We were going to the mental health facility to file a restraining order that would allow the police to pick Grant up if he was not willing to seek help on his own.

My heart ached as I tried to swallow the giant lump in my throat. *How did this happen? How did I miss the signs? What kind of wife am I? And what if he never comes home?* All of these thoughts tumbled through my mind as I tried to keep my feet in motion. What if I never heard his voice again? Or felt the warmth of his arms around me? Or what if I never felt the sweetness of his lips brush against mine? And as awful as any of them: What if I had to explain to my children that their Daddy was never coming home? My heart sagged under these burdens, and I kept begging God to show me what to do.

And then I saw them and froze mid-stride. Moving across the yard and all around Martha's truck were figures that I immediately knew to be angels. *Angels?* They completely surrounded the truck. "Martha, do you see them? Do you see the angels?" I asked as I climbed into the truck.

She glanced over at me, "No, I don't see anything."

I smiled, "They are all around the truck. They are carrying us." The briefest flash of hope stole across my heart. Maybe God was in this after all? But if He was, then why?

12:30pm

That was useless, I complained internally! The Bexar County mental health facility was a complete waste of time. We could process paperwork that would only guarantee Grant's safety temporarily. Even with that, there was no guarantee when he would be picked up, and by whom. If he did come home, I could not imagine waiting on pins and needles for some officer of the court to come and pick him up at some random time. Or worse, whether he was at work or at home I did not want to dishonor him through any kind of public humiliation. *I can't do this!*

I stood in the parking lot of the mental health office with sweat dripping down my back. The blood rushed wildly around in my head as I tried to decide what to do. Which was worse? Not having any kind of plan or committing myself to something that I wasn't sure would work.

Somewhere in the blackness of my mind I remembered an inpatient facility called Laurel Ridge. *Would they take him?* It turned out they would take him, but they couldn't keep him unless he voluntarily committed himself. *Great!* Like that was going to happen. But it was better than nothing…and all we had to go on at the moment. It was a gamble for sure, but one I was willing to take. What else were we supposed to do?

1:00pm

Poor Martha. Her phone didn't stop ringing all day. I knew she was trying to keep me from exhausting my fractured senses any more than necessary, but I felt bad for her. We sat across from each other at Whole Foods while she ate a sandwich and I sipped a smoothie. My sister Laura rang my phone. I decided to give Martha a break and took the call.

Laura was frantic. Her voice rang in my ear as she hammered me with question after question. Immediately I regretted taking the call. I tried to focus on the things she was saying but felt myself slipping into a dark cave of despair. *I can't handle this.* I hung up on her.

In the next few minutes every single member of my family called, wanting some kind of update. I watched Martha deal confidently with my siblings and my parents. I was amazed by her strength and fortitude. She was definitely handling this way better than I was, that's for sure.

A plan took shape as we headed home. My children were taken care of after school and I was ordered to get some rest. My Dad was coming in after dinner. I would pick him up with the kids and make up some kind of tale about how he and Grammie just couldn't stay away—they missed us so much. Martha would come back to my house to talk with my Dad and go over everything I had collected from the computer. We would have an appointment at Laurel Ridge the next day. And somehow we were going to figure out what flight Grant was coming home on Wednesday night.

7:00pm

"Hey guys, can you see him? There he is. Here comes Papa!" Zach and Kayla squealed in delight as they ran into his outstretched arms. They bombarded him with questions about why he was here, and when was Grammie coming in. Kayla looked up at him, "Papa, did you bring me anything?"

He smiled down at her, "Just a giant bear hug!" It was so great to see him. I choked back tears and walked into his arms...and felt safe for the first time that day. I breathed him in and was strengthened by his presence. He corralled the kids, gathered his luggage, and announced he was hungry. "Do you think we could get a burger on the way home?"

I laughed out loud. He had always been a fan of

cheeseburgers. Without missing a beat, Zach quipped, "What about a milkshake too?" Who knew that simple things could bring me so much joy?

9:30pm

Martha and Dad had just finished their discussion. I hugged Martha as she walked out the front door for the second time that day. "Allison, it's going to be okay." I tried to smile at her, but I wasn't so sure. I was able to gather from the flurry of phone calls that my family members weren't so sure either. "Martha, I don't think he's dead. I can't tell you why, but I don't think he is."

"I don't think he is either; he wouldn't have left you so many clues."

"You're right. And, if I know one thing about him, when he sets a plan in motion he sticks to it. What was the date on the letter?" I still hadn't read it.

"August 19," she replied. "Do you think he was intending to go to Atlanta, pick up the motorcycle, and just not come back?"

I wondered out loud, "His tickets for Atlanta were for the 19th so maybe he was going to mail it, pick up the motorcycle, and then…" I stopped. It made perfect sense. He had told me over the weekend that he was going to pick up the motorcycle and drive it home. He wasn't going to make it home from that trip. He was going to crash the motorcycle with himself on it.

"Martha, he's going to come home from this Dallas trip. I feel sure of it now. I think he's going to carry out his suicide plan on the way home from Atlanta." I told her what I was thinking, and she quickly caught on.

"Well, maybe." I could see the wheels turning in her head. She was being careful to not give me false hope. But I knew if we could just get him home, maybe we could get him help, save him, and save our marriage in the process. "I guess we are going to have to wait and see," she grimly replied. "Yeah, I guess so."

10:00pm

I took comfort in the knowledge that I wasn't alone in the house that night. As I got ready for bed, it felt good to know that my dad was waiting for me out in the living room. I knew he wanted to talk with me for a few minutes. I wasn't sure what he was thinking, but I wanted to make sure he knew how much I appreciated him being there.

We sat down on the couch together, and he smiled the smile he uses when he's trying to be kind. "Dad, thank you for coming, I didn't know what else to do." I looked over at him as tears again blurred my vision.

He reached over and hugged me, kissing me on the cheek. He whispered in my ear, "There isn't anything that could have kept me away." Then he tucked me into my bed, just like when I was a little girl.

I watched him walk away, and cried out, "Dad, do you think you could stay with me for a few minutes? Do you think you could tell me about when I was a little girl?" My lips trembled at that last part. I could not imagine feeling any smaller than I did at that moment.

He plopped down on the bed and began stroking

my hair. His voice was filled with melancholy and what I knew was the sound of love. "Of course I'll stay, honey. Until you fall asleep, and then I'll go pick up your mom from the airport. Remember?" Yes, of course I remembered, I was so thankful to have my Mom coming in that night. I knew they would both be able to help me figure this mess out.

He picked up my hand and began to tell me sweet memories of when I was a child. He filled my head with silly stories of my stubbornness. How I would stick my chin out and march across the yard when I was angry. How I used to go skinny dipping in our little play pool when I thought no one was looking. He told me how precious I was to him, and how I would always be his little girl. He told me how my sensitive heart touched him in ways that no one else did, and how thankful he was to have a little girl just like me. I fell asleep to that voice, knowing that I wasn't alone...and believing for that moment that maybe I was loved.

2:30am Wednesday

"Get away from me! Get away from me!" I'm screaming, but it's not helping. There are demons all around me. I'm surrounded and throwing my fists into as many as I can, to keep them from getting any closer. I kick and hit and scream louder, but no one is coming. They move closer, leering at me as my cries grow weaker. I open my mouth to scream at them but nothing comes out. They are on me now and I'm suffocating, I'm gone.

My eyes flew open as I bolted upright in bed. My head was reeling and I couldn't move my mouth without sending an excruciating stab of pain up the side of my cheek. Somehow my hand found my cheek, and I rubbed it, expecting it to be bloody. My eyes strained against the darkness. I couldn't see anything, but I knew they were there. Watching and waiting to see what I was going to do now.

I tried to lie back down in my bed, willing myself to sleep. But I couldn't. I was cold, my entire body shivering. I pulled the blankets higher and tried fiercely to stop shaking. But my breath came in gasps and fear compressed my chest. My heartbeat would not slacken, and the adrenaline surged on through my veins. *You're okay; you're all right. It was just a dream.* But I didn't believe myself. I could still hear the taunting voices in their horrific tones.

A tremendous evil boiled up from my stomach, filling my chest, then my mouth. I fought the urge to vomit, opening my mouth to scream, but nothing came out except a whimper. *I have to get out of here!* I threw off the covers and dashed to the bedroom door. But I felt the drag like hell's claws on my feet, pulling me backwards.

Miraculously I made it to the stairs. My parents were only feet away, and if I could make it to them, I knew the taunting would stop. Hot coals pushed volcanic heat through my body as I struggled forward. I could see their bedroom door now. *Just a few more steps. Come on…you can do this.*

At their bedside my chest heaved and sweat

trickled down my face. Every bone in my body ached. I opened my mouth to speak but could only utter an inhuman grunt as I collapsed onto their bed, aware of beast-like cries all around me. The ragged edges of reality seemed to slip from my grasp, and I shuddered beneath the weight of blackness that suffocated me. My parents wrapped me up in their arms, shielding me from those hellish voices, and I clung to them terror stricken, finally recognizing the beastly cries as my own.

I lost myself that night. In all my 35 years never had I experienced such tremendous grief at such a visceral level. I knew I was teetering dangerously on the edge of reality, and I clung to any sliver of hope that presented itself to me. There was no way of knowing what the morning would bring; I could only hope through my anguished cries that somehow God would intervene and have mercy on me and my family. Through some supernatural act, Grant would come home. All I could do was wait.

7:30am

I felt someone stir next to me and heard someone else out in the kitchen. And then I remembered how I had struggled up the stairs to my parents' room, collapsing on their bed. I remembered the three of us moving into my giant king size bed and them holding me as I wept. I had begged my mom to tell me about when I was a little girl and remembered the comfort her words brought. And then I remembered that my husband was gone on a suicide mission, and I didn't know if he was coming home.

I closed my eyes, willing myself back to sleep. I wasn't ready to wake up; my head throbbed like a bass drum, and it wasn't a hang-over. I looked over at my dad, saw that he was awake and mumbled something about going out to get some coffee. His arms moved out from under the covers and pulled me into a bear hug. "I love you Allison," he whispered as he patted my head. My eyes filled with tears as I melted into him.

"Thanks, Dad. I love you too."

Mom was drinking her tea as I rounded the corner into the kitchen. I warmed at the sight of her and quickly walked over and sank into her lap. She wrapped her arms around me as I rested my head on her shoulder. "Mom, I don't think I can do this." Her hands made circles on my back as she held me.

"Honey, we're sure going to try." I breathed her in as she held me. I loved the way she was so confident and sure. She had always been a source of emotional strength for me, and I hungrily drank in all she had to offer me.

"Allison, do Zach and Kayla have any idea what's going on?"

I thought for a minute before I replied. "I really don't think so. I told them you guys just couldn't stay away and for all they know, that's the truth." I smiled at her, "They think you worship the ground they walk on; what harm is there in letting them think that's why you're here?"

She laughed. "Well, they are pretty sweet, and I

wasn't planning on telling them anything, especially when we don't really know what we are dealing with yet." I nodded my head in agreement as I sat up and looked at her. I needed for both my parents to understand how desperate I was to protect the kids from whatever was coming.

"Mom, I really think the best thing we can do for them at this point is keep their schedules as normal as possible with the added benefit of you and Dad here for a visit. I can't imagine anything more than that right now. I can't imagine having to tell them..." My voice trailed off as I couldn't find the words to express the terror in my heart. "Mom, what if...? What if he's really not coming home?" I searched her face for the truth, wondering if she believed he was already gone.

Hearing the desperation in my voice, she pulled me in closer. "Honey, you and the kids are going to be okay. I know you want to protect them; I do too. That's why we're here: to help you, to love you, and to get this thing figured out. We just have to take it one thing at a time."

I sank back as thoughts swirled around my head. I knew she was right. There wasn't anything they wouldn't do for me. My parents were selfless when it came to their children, and I felt safe wrapped in Mom's arms, not unlike the many mornings I had spent sitting with her as a child. I was loved, and for that moment I felt hopeful.

1:00pm [Laurel Ridge Inpatient Facility]
There was no one in the waiting area, and yet I felt

the exposure of my naked soul as I sank into the soft upholstered chair. The receptionist smiled warmly as she invited me and my parents to wait for the intake counselor. *Was that pity I saw in her eyes? I don't need your pity! There is nothing wrong with me!* I closed my eyes and caught my breath. Anger swelled inside my head, exacerbating the throbbing that continued since the previous night. *How many people come here searching for an answer? How many people actually find it? How have I become one of them?*

The intake counselor ushered the three of us into her sparsely-decorated office. I clasped and unclasped my anxious hands, waiting for her to read through the papers I had printed and the suicide letter Grant had left. Periodically she would glance over at me, her gaze penetrating, her mind calculating.

I wonder what she's thinking.

I held my breath, hoping, praying that she would confirm it was all a big misunderstanding. She glanced at me, and then looked purposefully at my parents. "We have a significant problem, and I think you already know that." She paused and shifted her gaze to me, "Mrs. Johnson, do you understand?"

I shifted uncomfortably in my seat. *Do you think if I understood, I would be sitting here, listening to you, waiting for you to tell me what to do? Don't you think if I got it, and knew how to bring my husband home, I would be moving heaven and earth right now instead of listening to you?* "I'm not sure I know what you mean."

I forced myself to hold her gaze. She was intimidating, but I knew I needed to hear what she had to say. "Your husband is planning to kill himself and is planning to do it very soon…if it hasn't already happened. If he comes home, you need to get him into treatment immediately." She went on, "Based on everything I have seen here today, he is dangerously depressed, and definitely suicidal."

Words like, "containment," "restraining order," and "hospital stay" were thrown around casually like we were talking about what to order off the lunch menu. She was the hospital maitre d' offering the specials of the day, hoping we would make our selections so she could move on to the next unsuspecting group arriving with their desperation.

I closed my eyes and choked back the anguish that crept up my throat. The counselor explained that if we didn't get him into treatment willingly, we should call the police and they would come to my house, arrest him in front of my children, and throw him into a police car. *Like a common criminal? I wanted to scream!* The police would take him to Laurel Ridge, but they could not keep him unless he committed himself; even then it would only be for a short stay, a weekend at the most.

I shook my head fiercely when she looked pointedly at me, waiting for my response. "No, involving the police has to be the final option. I can't do that. I don't care what else we have to do, but I can't do that to him." I struggled to contain myself as I looked across the desk at her. "I will do whatever it takes to get him the treatment that he needs, but I can't do that. I just can't." I looked at my parents begging them to support me. Both of them met my gaze and a silent understanding communicated between us. We would do whatever it took; involving the police was the last option on the list.

How do you turn loose of a dream? For that matter, how do you even know when to turn loose and when to hold on for dear life? What do we genuinely have control over in this world? Not a whole lot, it seems to me. But I have learned a few things about dreams.

I have learned that dreams are what keep us connected to our hearts and make us feel alive, allowing us to believe that good will prevail and that happily ever after really does exist. I built my life with Grant on these hopes, believing that we were going to be in this world together, and when our time was up we would ride off into the sunset on a Harley Davidson motorcycle…together!

These dreams of a life together were torn out of my hands by a vicious, invisible ogre that crushed my hope. But now I know my dreams were only pushed aside for a season so that my hope would deepen, my love would grow, and my resolve would be strengthened. I learned that it's okay to let go, trusting that if my dream is God's dream too, then it will come around again, bigger and better than before.

Letting go of a dream is risky. It takes a leap of faith because not every specific dream does come back around; some are lost forever. Sometimes the marriage doesn't survive or a partner leaves despite the hardest efforts of the other. In cases like that, God seems to allow one dream to be lost...only to replace it with another. In these times, it's hard to see God at work, creating something from nothing or changing something that was ugly into something beautiful.

CHAPTER THREE

Who Are You?

My sweet, sweet love.
Where have you gone?

The darkness consumes you.
You are lost to me.

Find your way again,
Come back to me.

My love, come home.

"Blessed are those who mourn, for they shall be comforted." Matthew 5:4

4:00pm [Home]

It would be so easy to slip away. Walk out the door into another life, become another person, be someone who is stronger, more confident...free? Could I? *This is not the life I want; can I start over?* I wondered these things as I stood at the kitchen sink in the house I loved so much. I took in the carefully-painted faux finishes, the color-coordinated sofa, the chairs and coffee table I had chosen when we moved into this place three years earlier.

"Allison?" My Dad's voice interrupted my grim thoughts, "Al, I talked to the airline; Grant is scheduled to arrive on a 5:15 flight. He has already checked in." And then, "He's coming home." His words embraced me with the briefest recollection of hope. But what should have thrilled me didn't. My heart pounded as a dreadful fear gripped me. I can't do this. God I can't do this, I'm not strong enough, I'm afraid, please help me!

"Dad, couldn't I go with Mom, and you stay here? I'm really afraid." I pleaded with him earnestly, but I knew the answer. I had to do this, it was the only way.

"I know you're scared honey, but let's stick to the plan." He smiled at me as he walked to the kitchen table and planted himself in a wooden chair. "We're going to make this work. Remember what we talked about," he said gently.

"Alright," I relented, "But I'm still afraid." I sank into one of the wooden chairs next to him and reviewed the plan we had put together. Mom was taking the kids to Target and then to Red Robin for dinner. They wouldn't come home until I called them. Grant's friend Rob was on a flight to arrive at 9:40 that evening. Dad was going to shadow Grant, not letting him out of his sight, and talk him into getting help. If Grant fought us, or didn't agree to treatment or at worst left the house, Dad would follow him in my car, and I would have to call the police. It was risky, but one part of the puzzle was already solved: He was on his way home, and that was an answer to prayer.

6:10pm

I shifted in my seat and glanced at the clock, willing the hands forward. I laid my head in my arms on the oak table and tried to quiet the noise in my head. I thought of all the years we had known each other, more than half my life. And suppressed a smile as I thought of the first time we met twenty two years earlier in 7th grade gym class.

Not the most romantic setting for future lovers to meet but then again when I met him I knew there was no way I was going to be interested in him. Little did I know, he had been watching me for a few weeks and God had already planted the seed in his heart that I was the girl for him.

I think I was obnoxious to him that day but I don't have any memories that would confirm that. Grant remembers every detail, however, right down to the color of my tennis shoes. He says I was cute and sassy. He says I was a fiery, energetic little thing who intrigued him. I have to take his word for it since I don't remember any of it except that my shirt was yellow.

When people ask how we met I let him tell the story because it's fun to hear him talk about me with amusement and interest. And I suppose I like it that even as an adolescent I was attractive to him. I've tried to conjure up my own images of that fateful day but wind up using the pictures he has created for me instead. It was fall, I do know that, and I know that we were in gym class because he told me, but beyond that my memory is empty.

He says he followed me that day from the gym to the weight room with his friend Dave at his heels. After trying to hurry him up, Grant had taken off without him from the locker room and Dave apparently was quite annoyed. Weight lifting was Grant's thing and he used that excuse with Dave that day. He was in a hurry to get out there, and told Dave as much. "Its weight training day, it's my thing." Dave always laughed at him when he talked like that but Grant didn't care. He plowed his way through the crowd of guys heading for the gym. Yes, Grant loved weights but he knew if he told Dave the real reason he was in a hurry he would never hear the end of it. Grant had his eye on me and today was the day he was determined we would meet.

It was my neon yellow shirt that caught his eye. The first time he saw me that day I was wearing a yellow shirt and laughing at something my girl friend Jayme was saying. I had to cover my mouth to keep from giggling as Mr. Carlson began giving directions for proper weight training technique. I don't know how he did it but Grant somehow managed to maneuver himself closer to me as our class moved from each piece of equipment to the next. He says he could hear Mr. Carlson droning on and on about things like technique, body alignment, and no horseplay but he wasn't really paying attention. I guess he was distracted by me but I still find that hard to believe.

Once he finally reached his destination which was to stand right behind me, he admired how my hair lay in soft waves around the back of my neck. He could tell by the way I tilted my head that I was listening intently to the teacher. He says I still do that when I'm concentrating on something, even now.

When our teacher gave us the direction to partner up and make our rounds with the weight circuit Grant followed me with the sole purpose of being my partner. His plan would have worked if Dave hadn't yelled at him, "Hey Grant, where are you going?" At the same time he knocked Grant on the back of the head in the way that seventh grade boys did.

Grant whirled around to shut him up, but it was too late. I had stopped abruptly, and Grant bumped right into me. He threw his hands out to steady himself using my shoulders for balance. I spun around with my eyes flashing irritation and I shook his hands off with disgust saying something like, "Why don't you watch where you're going!"

Grant tried to smile at me as he said, "Hey, sorry about that," but he was too distracted by the slogan sprawled across the front of my t-shirt: *Pepsi Let Your Taste Decide!* He laughs now whenever he thinks about this since he ended up staring at my chest wondering what the slogan meant. Apparently I tolerated his staring by glaring back at him demanding, "What are you staring at?" Clearly he was blinded by love already because he says it was the sweetest voice he had ever heard. Even though I don't remember that moment I'm pretty sure that my voice was far from sweet.

We stood there staring at each other until he found the courage to introduce himself.

"My name is Grant and this is my friend Dave." Before I answered him I defiantly crossed my arms over my chest practically shouting at him, "Stop staring at me!"

The only thought that floated across his mind was *Wow, she's sassy!*

Because I was polite I introduced myself to him, "I'm Allison, Allison Rouse. It's nice to meet you." And then I turned and marched away from him.

He decided I was cute, had a nice smile and was definitely sassy. But there was something more, something fiery and tough. The way I looked at him had caught him off guard, stirring him up inside. He says more than ever he wanted to know me and hoped he would get the chance. I don't think either one of us knew that we would become great friends. I know we never would have imagined that someday one of us would be fighting to save the other's life.

The rustling pages of Dad's magazine brought me back to the present. Lifting my head to squint at the clock I registered the time. It was 6:10. He should be here any minute, I was sure of it. Dad glanced over his glasses and gave me a penetrating stare, "Are you okay? You're awfully fidgety over there."

"Well, what did you expect?" I snapped. "My butt hurts, I'm tired of sitting here, and did you forget that we are trying to save someone's life?" I bristled with tension and then immediately apologized for barking at him. "Dad, I'm sorry...it's just..." I stopped. The garage door was opening; the roar of Grant's BMW filled the garage as he pulled his car inside. He was home. He was home!

I leapt out of my chair starting for the door and then I remembered: This was no ordinary homecoming. He might not be happy to see me, and I couldn't embrace him with a hug and kiss like I normally did. I had absolutely no idea what to expect as he walked through the kitchen door.

He looked like he hadn't slept for days, or if he had, he had slept in his clothes. His eyes were red rimmed and his chambray shirt and khaki Dockers uncharacteristically rumpled. He dropped his keys on the counter as our eyes met across the kitchen. "Hi," I whispered as I stood up. Smiling weakly he nodded looking at me with tired eyes.

His face paled as he saw my dad for the first time. "What are you doing here?" He looked at me with confusion as I walked over to him. Putting my arms around his waist I hugged him briefly before he moved away. He turned to face me, "What's going on Allison? Why is your dad here?"

Swallowing my fear, I reached out and squeezed his hand, "Honey, I am very concerned about you. I asked my dad to come down and help me. You left me some things that made me worry about how you are, and I thought maybe he could help." My voice cracked as I choked back the words I wanted to scream at him. *Where were you? What's happening to you? Are you okay?*

With a sigh he looked at my dad, then back at me. Turning on his heel, he marched out of the kitchen, saying as he passed, "I see. Well, that's fine. I'm going to work out."

I shot Dad a look of desperation as I watched my husband walk farther away from me. Dad nodded and followed him out of the room. *Good, he's going to stay with him,* I thought, as I leaned my weary head on the counter. *At least he's home; that's an answer to prayer....* But it was anyone's guess how the rest of the night would go. I prayed fervently, hoping God would intervene and rescue us from this nightmare. We had a long way to go.

I positioned myself at the bottom of the staircase once I heard them upstairs. I could make out bits and pieces of their conversation while the sound of the stair climber whirled in the background. I rested my head against the railing, willing my ears to work overtime. I wanted to move closer, but there was no way I was going to risk interrupting them.

Hearing their footsteps drum down the hallway, I ran to my post in the kitchen and nonchalantly poured myself a glass of water. I waited. Was it really going to be as straightforward as having a conversation about treatment, Grant agreeing, and then living happily ever after? I hoped so...but even though I'm an optimist at heart, I don't always believe my own fairytale.

Dad walked into the kitchen behind Grant, giving me the thumbs up sign. *Really?* I thought incredulously. Grant poured himself a glass of water, and I waited. It was all I could do to keep from shouting, "What happened?"

Dad poured himself a Diet Coke and settled himself next to the refrigerator. Grant stood at the counter, sweat dripping down the slope of his neck as he lifted his glass for a long drink. My heart beat in my throat as I thought of all the times I had kissed that neck. Even now, in the middle of the biggest crisis of our lives I longed to be next to him. I wanted to cradle him in my arms, hugging him close, breathing my life and my love into him,

Dad spoke first, "Grant has agreed to call Dr. Young and talk with him about seeing a psychiatrist. He realizes that he needs to get this thing figured out and so we agreed that he would do that tonight." He paused, looking over at Grant before he continued. "I told him that Rob was coming in tonight and that we are all here because we love him, and are concerned for him and for your family."

I couldn't keep my eyes off Grant while my dad's words washed over me. Grant avoided my gaze and simply nodded his head. He reached out, picked up the phone, and dialed Dr. Young's number.

Hearing Grant's voice as he spoke to his doctor soothed my worn-out nerves as it often had over our twelve years of marriage. It always sounded sweet and pure; it flowed into the hollow places within me, touching my heart, warming my soul. All of a sudden I felt elated. I wanted to dance inside my warm little kitchen. Hope bloomed…and the feeling of terror that had encased my heart was replaced with love and tenderness. It was going to be okay; we were going to get this thing worked out. I had to believe that. I wanted to believe that. Grant clicked the phone off, turning to face me and my dad. His lips held a firm line making me wonder if he would ever smile again.

"Dr. Young says he's taken me as far as he can, he wants to turn me over to a colleague of his. He's a psychiatrist here in town and is supposed to be a good one." Clearing his throat he continued, "He says that I need to get seen right away and he's afraid if I don't that I could end up in the hospital. It's pretty obvious that the antidepressants I've been taking aren't working anymore or at all so he is going to make some calls for me and hopefully I'll be able to get in with this new doctor by the end of the week." He poured the last of the water out of his glass, letting his words sink in before he continued. "Dr. Peterson is supposed to be really good so...I guess we'll just have to see what he says." He leaned into the counter for support, crossing his arms across his chest, as if to hold himself together. Shaking his head, he looked at the floor and repeated to himself, "I guess we'll just have to see what he says."

I was skeptical but kept my doubts to myself, and as much as I wanted to take him to the emergency room right then and there, I forced myself to trust the doctor who had cared for him up to now. He was a good one. And by the time his nurse called us back with the appointment with Dr. Peterson for Friday evening, I had almost convinced myself we were on the right track. Two days did seem like a very long time, but I knew that if anything changed Mom and Dad would help us figure out what to do.

Later after the kids had gone to bed, and Rob had been picked up from the airport, I spread peanut butter and jelly across the buttermilk bread that Zach and

Kayla loved so much. Yes, focus on the simple things, I thought, and smiled as I imagined them shoving their sandwiches into their mouths as fast as possible letting the jelly dribble down their chins like they always did. They were such sweet kids, if only we could figure this out and be a family again. Sealing the sandwiches tightly into their plastic I imagined sealing my heart into its own Ziploc bag, only to be opened again when it was ready to be shared.

Mom laid her hand on my shoulder interrupting my thoughts, "Al, you should really get some rest." I shrugged her off. I knew I needed to go to bed, but I wanted to see Grant when he got home. After I picked up Rob they had gone for a drive, and they weren't back yet. He hadn't really spoken to me since his homecoming, and I felt a familiar knot of fear growing deep inside. He was angry at me! I knew it. Even though things had gone amazingly well since Grant had talked to Dr. Young, and everyone else seemed encouraged, I wasn't. I had to see him, had to know he was home.

"Mom," I turned to look at her. "Do you think we are doing the right thing? Do you think we should have taken him to the hospital?" I was feeling scared again. What if we were only prolonging the inevitable?

"Al," she paused, "I'm not sure." She knelt down, wiping up water from the dishes I was putting away. She studied her wet cloth for a moment before she continued, "I don't think there is any way we can know for sure that we have done the right thing until he sees the doctor. You heard that he has an appointment on Friday with a new doctor. In the meantime I think you should get some rest."

Yeah, the doctor was supposed to be a good one. But I wanted him there now. Today! Not Friday. I certainly didn't want him going to work tomorrow which he declared he had to do. I shook my head. I just wasn't sure. Maybe it was the exhaustion kicking in, but I couldn't help feeling nervous about letting him out of my sight. He was good at pretending, and I wasn't sure I trusted him to keep his word at this point.

"Okay," I smiled at her, "I'll go to bed, and are you sure you're good with getting up with the kids."

"Of course, I wouldn't have it any other way." She swatted me on the bottom as I walked slowly out of the kitchen. I was so glad they were here.

I didn't recognize myself as I washed my face. Purple circles were embedded beneath my brown eyes, and fine lines were making themselves at home at the tops of my freckled cheeks. It had been a long time since I felt so exhausted. Maybe since childbirth...but even then it felt different. With childbirth there was joy and elation at the end of the exhaustion. This exhaustion was soul emptying, cutting me to the core of my being, leaving me helpless and bereft, cold and alone. I fell asleep wondering if God would hear me if I prayed, knowing I was too tired to care. I fell asleep thinking of a time seventeen years earlier as seniors in High School that Grant and I were friends and I had wished with the depth of any school girl crush that we would someday be way more than just friends.

It was fall that day when I slammed my locker door and moved into the crowd of students rushing to their classes. Too late...I knew I was going to be late. Four minutes is definitely not enough time to get to class, I thought grumpily as I bumped my way through the throng of kids. I searched the crowd for Grant. Ever since we had briefly dated over the summer I couldn't help but think about him. Over the years our friendship had grown. He was fun and I liked him a lot. I had never met anyone that was so genuine, and seemed to sincerely care about me.

I smiled at people I knew, offering a friendly hello. The stack of books grew heavier in my arms as I entered the hallway that held my History class. Finding Mr. Bergevin's class I made my way through the door and tumbled into my seat. The tardy bell rang and I breathed a sigh of relief. I had made it, barely. Grant turned in his seat and smiled kindly. "Hi," he whispered flirtatiously. "You just made it."

I nodded quickly, avoiding Mr. Bergevin's stare, "I know, lucky me." Grant turned away, leaving me to stare at the muscles in his back that rippled under the threads of his cotton t-shirt. *He's so cute! I wish we were still dating!* I shifted in my seat and daydreamed of the way he would hold my hand or kiss me softly. I had fallen for him, hard. There was no denying it, but he had moved on and I was left with my secret crush.

At least I can stare at him and he won't know it, I thought miserably. I had only these fifty minutes to sit behind him, staring at the waves of blonde hair that curled around his head, and to hope that he might turn around and flash me his devilish grin. I imagined him taking me in his arms, staring deep into my eyes and professing his undying love for me. I shook my head, and opened my history book. This was not helping. I made up my mind to find a way to get over him, but I had no idea how.

"Allison. Allison? Can you hear me? Allison, it's me, Rob. Grant has something he wants to say to you." I snuggled deeper into the pillows clinging to that day in history class when life was simpler and I could feel new love in its purest most innocent form. But again Rob's voice dove into my dreaming and I forced myself to open my eyes. "Allison, Grant needs to talk to you. Can you please wake up?"

Blinded by the hallway light I struggled to recognize the voice calling my name. I was able to make out Rob standing at my bedside, Grant filled in the space behind him. I pushed myself up on my pillows, pushing the remnants of sleep deeper into the darkness of my brain. I glanced at the clock. 12:15? *How come he wants to talk to me now,* I wondered as I stared into the face of the man I loved. *What could he possibly want to say to me?*

"Allison," he lay down on the bed next to me and picked up my hand. I wanted to jerk it away, but I was hypnotized by his voice. His eyes searched mine and then he spoke again, his voice like sugar pouring softly over my aching body. "Allison, I'm sorry. I didn't mean to hurt you, and I'm just so very sorry." His voice broke as he lowered his lips to gently kiss my hand, and then encased it in both of his.

Really? He was sorry? Sorry for what? For making me think he was dead? Or for the cruel things he said to me? Tears spilled down my cheeks as I stared at his chiseled nose and felt his hazel eyes pierce through the walls around my heart. As much as I wanted to be angry with him, I felt it slipping away. My heart burned with desire for him, even as my inner voice told me to be afraid.

It took all of my will to crush the doubts that consumed me. I couldn't imagine life without him, and if he was sorry then I would forgive him. We would get through this, and our lives would move on. He took me in his arms then, holding me close as I sobbed against his shoulder. I gave my heart back to him in that moment, not knowing what I was giving up...or if I would ever be the same again.

Rolling over the next morning, I opened my eyes and caught a glimpse of my clock radio. The light overwhelmed my sleep-deprived eyes, and I quickly squeezed them shut again. *How did it get to be noon already? Had I really been asleep for twelve hours?*

I sat up in bed, threw the covers off, and stormed into the bathroom. I stood there examining myself in the mirror and wondered if it was something I had done. The person that looked back at me from the mirror was a stranger. She stood lifeless, her shoulders drooped and her eyes stared blankly into nothingness. Overnight I had fallen into a black pit, and I had no idea how to get out.

I heard a tiny voice inside my head, *"I hate this."* I nodded at myself in the mirror. Yes, I know I hate this.

The voice grew stronger until its sound pulsed through my veins... *I hate this! I hate this! I hate this!* Tearing open the bedroom door, I tried to stop the voices screaming inside my head. I fought with them as I marched toward the kitchen, barely recognizing the voices of my parents and Rob. All three of them looked up at the same time as I marched into the kitchen. I paused breathless at the kitchen sink, bowing my head to avoid their curious stares. I knew they would see how angry I was, and I was desperate to keep it together. Over the voices in my head I heard Dad clear his throat, "Um, good morning, Allison. How was your night?" An innocent question, but I was not prepared to answer it. Slowly I lifted my head to meet his gaze. A flicker of confusion came over his face as he recoiled from the venomous look I sent in his direction.

In a voice I did not recognize, I heard myself answer, "How the hell do you think my night was, Frank?" He stared back at me stunned. "I'll tell you how my night was: It was just great. Brilliant! Wonderful!" I played up the drama for shock value but felt unable to stop. I couldn't stop shaking as I found myself on the edge of reason, plummeting curiously close to the outer realm of my sanity. It felt exhilarating and terrifying at the same time.

"Allison, are you okay?" Mom asked in a concerned voice.

"Oh sure," I roared back. "I'm great; didn't you hear me? I just told Dad I had a great night so why wouldn't I be great. I mean, my husband tried to kill himself two days ago, and now he's at work." I spat the words in her direction. "At work, can you believe that? You three are sitting here; you've traveled all this way to help us, and he's at work!" I began to laugh hysterically. "Clearly work is sooo important, ha! Don't you see how this looks, how he's playing you?" I catch the look of confusion on Rob's face.

"Do you have any idea what this has been like for me? Do you!? I've barely slept for days, my kids have not seen me, and I feel like I might actually be losing my mind." I forced a sarcastic smile as they stared back at me. I figured they knew I was on a quick moving freight train, bound for disaster.

I lowered my voice as I quoted recent words from Grant, "It sucks being in a relationship with you Allison, and I don't want to be with you. You are the most selfish person I have ever known!" I paused and looked Dad right in the eye. "Do you have any idea how much I hate what he is doing to our life, what he's doing to me?"

My voice broke at that part and I started to cry. "I've tried everything I could possibly think of over the years to make him happy, to be the kind of wife he might want. But I don't think I can do this anymore. I really don't." I lowered my face and began to weep hysterically. My entire body shook as the exhilaration of anger was replaced with a sadness so heavy it felt like my body would collapse under its weight. I was sinking now, and all I could think about was how much I wanted to get out of there, how much I wanted to be any place else.

I heard a chair slide over the tiled floor and then

felt gentle hands begin to rub my back as I lay with my face buried in my arms. Tears mixed with snot pooled on the counter top. "Mom?" I whispered, carefully forming the words. I needed to know it was her.

"Yes, honey, I'm here." I wanted to crawl into her lap and be a little girl again, I wanted to lose myself, be someone else, to go away and never look back.

My voice quivered as fresh tears began to burn in my eyes, closing my throat with their weight. "Please, could we just go to the beach? Please?" I finally stood up to meet her gaze. My eyes pled with hers, searching for the answers, instead I found unconditional love mixed with a horrifying burden of sadness. Her eyes reflected what she saw in mine: a pain so great it was difficult to bear. I looked away, knowing we weren't going anywhere.

"Al?" Dad asked carefully. "Al, maybe this can be a fresh start for you two. Maybe this will be a good thing in the end." I couldn't agree. In fact his words just made me angrier.

I gripped my fists, willing them to stay at my sides and fighting the undeniable urge to hit someone, anyone. Taking a huge breath, I heaved at him, "I don't want a fresh start! Ahh!" I screamed in frustration, my fists punching the air. "Don't you see, don't you see? I just want my life back!"

I could hear them calling after me as I made my way past them to the patio door. I threw it open, jumped through, and slammed it behind me, shrieking at no one in particular, "I'm going to the beach!"

I sank into a patio chair and closed my eyes.

Images of my favorite beach began to flood the corners of my mind. The sound of the waves crashing on the sand quieted the voices of hate that had filled my head before. I could feel the sun warming my bitter soul, as the salty wind blew across my face, drying my tears as quickly as they fell. The beach had always been my oasis in the desert and the place where God spoke. This time proved to be no different, and in the months to come He would continue to meet me here, showing me I was not alone, carrying me through what would prove to be the most challenging and painful time of my life.

CHAPTER FOUR

Get Me Off This Roller Coaster!

"You will seek me and find me when you seek me with all your heart." Jeremiah 29:13

June 1990 [Colorado Springs]

The microphone crackled with static as General Hosmer, Superintendant of the US Air Force Academy, positioned himself behind the podium. Grant stood stiffly at attention and anticipated the words the General was about to speak. A cold front was rolling in off the Rocky Mountains, charging the freshman class with electricity that permeated the crowd. Before ever setting foot in a war zone, every man standing rigidly around him was battle-hardened, a survivor of roughly 365 days of battle to get to this place of victory and celebration. Now, a few words were all that separated my future husband and his classmates from becoming part of the human race again.

From the instant he had stepped off the bus to basic training, to this moment where he stood on the parade grounds waiting for recognition, not a second had gone by that he didn't feel like he was living in hell. He had endured constant hazing that bordered on insanity, sleep deprivation and upperclassmen trying to worm their way into the fortress that had become his mind. Others had withered under the intense, never-ending persecution...and Grant had vowed to not become one of them. The only respite that came his way was a small amount of sleep, but it was never enough. A glance at his own reflection reminded him that his lean physique was a direct result of the intense physical training he had received.

General Hosmer cleared his throat and seemed to pause dramatically as if enjoying this last moment of the freshman peasantry. Grant's skin buzzed as he waited for the words of freedom. The General's voice boomed across the parade field, "Freshman class of 1993, you are now recognized!" With a roar of celebration they clapped each other on the back and hit high fives all around. Grant's heart lifted as he realized the tremendous accomplishment he had just achieved. A group of them were going to celebrate up at Arnold Hall, but he could only think of one person he really wanted to share this with—me.

Striding up the parade ramp with the rest of his classmates, he wondered what I was doing. He hadn't spoken with me since his grandfather's death, seven months earlier. Even then it had only been a brief moment. Grant smiled to himself as he remembered the sound of my energetic voice and the smile that never failed to pierce his heart. In the midst of his class work and focus on football he daydreamed about the fun times we had spent together before we both graduated from high school and gone our separate ways. *Man I think I really miss her,* he thought. And realized there was still an emotional connection he felt, even across the miles. Somehow I still owned a piece of his heart. Of all his friends, he believed that only I would understand the significance of this monumental day for him. He was on top of the world, and he wanted to share the experience with me.

August 19, 2005

"Not what you had planned?" Robert asked me as I sank wearily onto the rose-colored sofa that flanked the opposite side of his office. I'd lost track of the number of visits I had paid him over the years. He was the only Christian family therapist I knew, and I came to him today hoping for some kind of encouraging word. I shook my head silently and closed my eyes for a moment before answering.

"No, definitely not what I had planned. I can't think, I can't sleep, and I can't wake up from this nightmare. What in the world am I supposed to do?" I laid my head on the back of the sofa, wishing the floor would open up and whisk me away to some place far away where my anguish and pain could not follow.

"Allison, can we just talk for a while about what has happened, and see where God leads?" Lifting my head to look at him, I decided it was worth a try. Wasn't that why I had come here? I nodded and grabbed a tissue. Slowly I began to re-tell the hellish events that had transpired over the last few days. I retreated inside myself as the words took on a life of their own. I could hear my voice speaking but found myself drifting to the beach again, crying out to God to save me, to please save my husband and to save my marriage.

"Allison?" Robert gently brought me out of my trance and I stared at him with tear-filled eyes. "You told me earlier that Grant was going to see the psychiatrist this afternoon. Has he ever been to a psychiatrist before?" I thought quickly of the awful scene at the Nix Hospital we had visited the summer before. *Wow, how could I have forgotten that?*

The Nix hospital was the closest I had ever come to being inside the psychiatric ward. It was cold, sterile, and smelled of antiseptic. Patients were locked behind heavy doors marked "No Entry," and periodically a cry or shriek would echo into the waiting room. It was a scary place, and the doctor who saw us was about as warm as a cadaver.

He had seemed disinterested, taking sporadic notes, as Grant expressed his fears about being depressed, of being out of control. When Grant began talking about his own brand of vigilante justice, which included throwing large pieces of wood stuck with nails beneath the tires of cars that had been drag racing through our neighborhood, the doctor sprang to life. He tapped his pencil on his knee impatiently but allowed Grant to finish and then he pounced, pronouncing a diagnosis of manic-depression/bipolar and urged him to admit himself to the hospital immediately for treatment.

"Robert, I can't believe I forgot about what happened last summer. He did go see a psychiatrist last summer. He asked me to find a psychiatrist for him, and I found one at the Nix."

"He asked you to find the doctor?" Robert asked clearly surprised.

"Yes, he did." I shook my head in disbelief, how could I have forgotten? "Geez, I can't believe I forgot about that. He had gone on a rampage in the neighborhood one night, and I think it scared him. We went to the Nix hospital together, but it was not a good scene." I quickly recounted that horrific experience for him as I sank protectively into the sofa cushions. How could I explain to him that we had been terrified and had pretty much run out of the hospital before they carried him off to the psych ward?

"I don't think we were ready to hear that diagnosis. It freaked us both out and we closed our minds to it. Maybe if we had paid attention and gotten him help then, things would have turned out differently. What do you think?" *Oh, how I wished things were different.*

Smiling at me, Robert began rubbing a cloth over his glasses. "Based on the things you have told me, it sounds like he is extremely clinically depressed, but...he is taking antidepressants." He paused to inspect the lenses a little more and went back to rubbing them furiously. "They aren't working for him, obviously." I smiled at his understatement as he continued. "If they were working for him, he wouldn't have gotten this far into the hole he's in now. It might be as simple as changing his antidepressants." Placing his glasses back on his cheeks he sat back in his chair, letting his words sink in.

"Allison, there is another option here, but I'm not a psychiatrist." He paused politely as I gestured for him to continue. "It's possible that Grant could be bipolar. That doctor might have been right, but I find it difficult to imagine he could diagnose him just like that, without any further time spent analyzing him."

"So are you saying that you think Grant is bipolar instead of just clinically depressed?"

"Allison, what I'm saying is he *could* be, but it's going to take some time to get it figured out. If he is bipolar the anti-depressants will not work for him, and he will get worse." *Worse? How could he possibly get any worse? He had just planned to commit suicide; was there anything worse than that?*

The familiar ache on the side of my cheek began to throb as I processed what he was telling me. I had known Grant to be depressed off and on over the course of our marriage but had never considered that it could be something more serious. Bipolar? What in the world did that even mean? My frazzled brain could not contend with this new idea, and the ache in my cheek expanded down into my jaw, tightening with every beat of my heart.

This was just too much! Depression I thought I could handle and navigate fairly well; bipolar, on the other hand...well, that was an entirely different universe, and I wasn't sure I wanted to go there. I couldn't imagine things getting worse than they already were. I had my doubts about my ability to handle anything more and began quietly weeping. Despair crawled over me as I wondered if my husband would ever be the same again.

Burying my face in my hands, I cried out to God. *Please help me.* I felt myself drifting back to the beach. It didn't seem right to escape there, and yet there was nothing I could do to keep it from happening. The salty breeze carved its way into my heart, filling me with warmth and serenity. I floated on the wings of angels who carried me towards the warmth of the sun, extinguishing the cries of my anguished soul.

"Robert, I think I might be losing my mind. I don't think I can take this anymore. I just really want to go to the beach in my mind right now. Can I please go to the beach? It makes me feel so much better, and I just need to be quiet for awhile. Sensing my fear, he looked at me for a moment before his rich voice broke through the internal sound of waves crashing onto foam-encrusted sand. "Allison."

"Yes."

"You can go to the beach as much as you want."

I smiled at Robert then, feeling the overwhelming weight of worry slip away. I let my spirit soar, carried into the surf of my imagination. I laid my head back against the sofa and images of our life together flashed across my mind. Images of our wedding day, and the time we went square dancing in high school and then that summer day in 1990 when he called me and I didn't know who he was. That was the beginning, the first time I knew he was reaching out to me and I was surprised at how good that felt.

"Allison, can you get the phone?" Mom had hollered at me from the kitchen, "My hands are all wet."

"Alright, I got it," I yelled back at her, my voice echoing off the high white ceiling of our basement. Throwing the pile of laundry I was folding into the basket, I quickly muted the TV and grabbed the telephone on what I thought was the final ring. "Hello."

"Hi. Is Allison there?" The caller's voice reached into the innermost part of my memory asking me to place it with a name.

"This is Allison, who is this?" The voice was becoming more familiar as I waited for his response, but still nothing jogged my memory.

"Allison, it's so great to hear you. It's me, Grant."

Without thinking I quickly retorted, "Grant who?"

"Grant Johnson." I could hear him smiling across the line. Of course, *Grant Johnson*. Wow, what was he doing calling me?

"Grant, I'm so sorry; it's just been such a long time. It took me a minute to recognize your voice. Where are you and what are you doing?" My mind raced even as butterflies flitted across my belly. Talk about a great surprise!

"Well, Ally…" he paused, letting his pet name for me sink in. I wanted to squeal; he was the only person who had ever called me that, and I loved it. "I just got recognized at the Air Force Academy. It's kind of a big deal and you were the first person I wanted to call."

Whoa, seriously? I was flattered but played it cool and asked him to tell me all about it. For the next fifteen minutes his voice poured over the line as he shared with me the amazing accomplishment he had just celebrated. I was honored that he wanted to share his excitement with me and told him so.

It felt so easy to be talking with him and reminded me of the great times we had enjoyed in high school, including the late night phone calls we used to share. "Ally, I'm going to be in town in a few weeks and would love to get together. Do you think we could?" He asked innocently. I wished I could jump through the phone and see him right then.

"Of course, just call me when you get to Yakima, and we'll set something up." I smiled to myself as we said our goodbyes. Hmmm. Mentally I calculated the days, I was surprised at how excited I was to see him and told myself to keep it cool. Who knew what he was thinking...maybe he just wanted to visit an old friend. Then again, maybe he wanted something more. Would I want something more? I didn't know the answer to that, but I promised myself I would find out.

In the meantime I had some work to do. I started folding laundry again as my mind drifted back to some of my favorite memories of him, our friendship, and the short time we dated. I could only hope the future would be as great.

As I think back to this tumultuous time, I can see now that I lived in a realm of denial that allowed me to create and believe an illusion of safety. My conscious mind only allowed me to process so much at any given point, but somewhere deep inside I knew my life was falling apart. I could see the truth but felt ill-equipped to handle it, so I took trips to the beach in my mind. It was part of my survival mechanism and a way that I could "time out" from the disturbing situation I was in.

Grief had gripped my state of being like a giant wave, and I was dangerously close to letting it shipwreck me. I spent my days trying to do normal things while I slowly retreated into myself. I wanted to hide from everyone and everything.... It was impossible to imagine being with people since I was in such pain and, to be honest, I felt ashamed. I felt like a failure and believed that Grant's illness was my fault. He had been so unhappy for so long that I related it to him being unhappy with me, our life, and our marriage. Why else would he not want to be alive anymore?

My rational mind could comprehend the staggering degree of depression and its effects on his life, but my emotions were clouded by a dark grief, causing me to believe that it was my entire fault. I'm thankful for my counselor who helped me see where I was and how to get out of that scary place. I visited him twice a week for many months before I felt like I could handle myself and my emotions.

To this day my favorite scripture verse is Jeremiah 29:11, "For I know the plans I have for you," declares the LORD, "plans to prosper you and not to harm you, plans to give you hope and a future." This passage helped me remember, when I was anxious and afraid, that God had good plans for me and that I could indeed hope for a renewed future.

Fall 2005

"Grant, I really want to go with you to the appointment today." I set down my hairbrush and reached for my toothpaste as I watched him finish shaving. I knew there was enough time for me to be ready, so I silently willed him to accept my request. I hadn't gone with him the first time, since Dad and Rob were here instead. Since that first appointment he seemed better, but I didn't really trust my instincts anymore and needed to hear it from the doctor myself.

"Why?" He said curiously, as he glided the razor over his throat creating a smooth patch of skin.

Why not? I thought as I struggled to find the words that would convince him of my need to go. I needed to feel like there was something to hope for and reached for some kind of connection with him. Instead, it felt like we were slipping farther and farther away from each other every day. That familiar sense of fear moved up the back of my neck. In the weeks since the intervention a wall had slowly emerged between us, and I was anxious to keep it from growing any higher.

"Honey, I just feel so confused, and I think it's important for Dr. Peterson to hear from me too. To help me understand what's been going on around here."

His eyes narrowed as he wiped his chin with a damp towel, cleaning remnants of shaving cream from his throat. I could tell he was thinking and so I waited to hear if I would be welcome or not. "Allison," he turned toward me with a piercing gaze. I took a step backward as he continued, "You can come if you want, but remember that this is my appointment, my doctor, and you can't say anything."

I wanted to scream. I was allowed to show up but couldn't talk, what did that mean? "Grant, I don't think I understand what you mean. Why can't I say anything? I live here; don't you think he needs to hear from me too? Besides, there are so many things I don't understand, things I *need* to understand."

My questions lingered in the air between us and then it clicked for me. He had made it pretty clear in the previous weeks that he didn't view the intervention I had coordinated as an act of love; in fact, he saw it as a clear violation of trust in our relationship. The very thought that I had even considered having him arrested and admitted to a mental hospital made him want to stay as far away from me as possible. He didn't want me to say anything at the appointment because he was trusting Dr. Peterson now for the way through this and feared the relationship fallout might get in the way of finding medical help. He *didn't* trust me right now...and there was nothing I could say or do to change it. No amount of pleading with him was going to change his mind. He was as angry with me as I was with him.

In spite of that, I knew as his wife I had a reason for being there. I needed to show support, and I needed to find some grain of truth that would ease my anxious mind. It was a place to start and I was willing to do whatever it took to re-establish something that felt familiar.

He whirled around, resentment creeping into his eyes as he firmly repeated, "You can come, but he's my doctor. He doesn't need to hear from you." I knew from the very first appointment Grant had with Dr. Peterson that their relationship of trust had grown significantly. Grant saw him as someone who really understood what was happening and trusted him to figure it out. They had built a very close working relationship as Grant religiously kept his appointments, which in turn, allowed Dr. Peterson to dive deeper into his diagnosis. Dr. Peterson had suspected bipolar as a diagnosis from that very first emergency appointment but protocol was to rule out depression first. It hadn't occurred to me that I wouldn't be part of the team in helping Grant get better. "He doesn't need to hear from you," he repeated making sure I got the message.

His words stung, but I clung to the hope that if I could at least hear from the doctor myself, perhaps some questions would be answered whether I got to say anything or not. "Fine, if that's how you want it." I replied as I furiously stuck my toothbrush in my mouth, managing to quiet my voice at the same time.

I don't care if he ever believes what I did was for him, I told myself as I focused on brushing each tooth with extra care. *He can think what he wants; there is nothing I can do to change that. He is still alive, still here, and that is going to have to be enough for me for now.*

Later at Dr. Peterson's office I listened to him speak very clearly about what we were trying to accomplish.

Dr. Peterson was pleased with Grant's progress but reminded us that it could take up to six months for the new antidepressants to fully take effect.

I had secretly been hoping Grant would start counseling with Robert and me immediately, but that was pushed out until after the New Year. According to Dr. Peterson, "It would not be productive until he is pulled up out of this fog." He encouraged us to keep from talking about anything of any extreme importance and cautioned me to be patient.

"These things take time, and I know you want what's best for him," he said looking directly at me. I nodded my head. *Of course I do, but what about what's best for me?*

Dr. Peterson used the analogy of two boxers staying in their corners during a time out. That was our task for the next six months, "Stay in your corners, don't come out swinging. Give yourselves the time out that you need. Then, when he's better, you can start counseling and work on repairing your marriage."

I could tell he was satisfied with his summary, and I left the appointment feeling a small bit of encouragement. I could stay in my corner. I was determined to make this work and wanted more than anything to show Grant how much I loved him and wanted him to get better. I would move heaven and earth to keep our family together. I would put my needs aside and focus on him, doing everything I could to make things right again. I imagined us getting through the next six months, and then somehow we would bridge the gap of pain and discover new love and new life together. I couldn't have been more wrong.

"Honey, wait up." I followed him out of the building trying to match his stride. He was irritated, and I was desperate to keep up with him. "Grant, please wait for me." He turned around giving me a flat look of defeat.

"What do you want," he growled.

Startled, I stumbled over my words. "Well...I...uh," I stopped. I didn't recognize him anymore and didn't know what to say. I just looked at him feeling as if the dam holding back my tears would break at any moment. Grunting at me, he walked over to his car and got in. I scrambled quickly into the passenger seat trying not to look at him; silently, I wondered what had gone wrong.

After that appointment, we fell into a routine of silent hostility, masked by our efforts to keep things as normal as possible for Zach and Kayla. The time we spent alone together was strained at best, punctuated by his mood changes that were often and unexpected. Days would pass as we barely spoke. I could have walked through the room naked, and he wouldn't have noticed, causing me to believe that it was only a matter of time before he would leave me for good.

And then like sunlight that warms the earth after a thunderstorm, his smile would permeate the cold, dark stare that gripped his face, briefly transforming him into the Grant I knew and loved. But I lived for those moments and fought with every ounce of my being to hang on to the dream of living happily ever after.

Time would be the only indication of any improvement made for Grant, for me, and for our marriage. The boundary between truth and illusion felt very slim, and I found myself searching for truth but doubting the result. I didn't trust myself, or Grant, and believed on some pathetic level that God had abandoned us.

I'm not sure when it happened, but one night I woke up realizing that the music in my heart was silent. I had no idea how long it had been gone, I felt abandoned, angry, and very, very alone. This music that resonated throughout my body had always been my link to God—in good times and in bad, the music had sustained me...and now it was gone. Why would God abandon me in my greatest hour of need? Why, when I needed him most, did I feel Him the least?

I went through the motions of daily responsibilities while I challenged God, searching my Bible to discover the promises he had made that he wasn't keeping. I was determined to prove that he had abandoned me, didn't love me, and was punishing me. Instead, what I found was scripture that was meant for me. I discovered Psalm 16:7 that reminded me that even at night my heart was being instructed by God. Psalm 139:5-6 told me that I was protected on all sides and that God's hand had been laid upon me. And perhaps the most powerful scripture of all, Isaiah 43:1-3: "Fear not, for I have redeemed you; I have summoned you by name; you are mine. When you pass through the waters, I will be with you; and when you pass through the rivers, they will not sweep over you. When you walk through the fire, you will not be burned; the flames will not set you ablaze. For I am the Lord, your God, the Holy One of Israel, your Savior…" (NIV)

My life was a mess, my husband was very sick, and I had to stop pretending that I knew what to do when I didn't. I thought that by challenging God I was protecting myself from getting hurt again. The truth is that I was wasting a lot of time and energy being mad at God when he was the only one who was able to help me. If I was going to survive, I had to stop trying to prove God was a liar and instead recognize that his truth was sovereign and ultimately good in my life.

I started reading my Bible with the attitude that God had something in mind for me and I wanted to know what that was. I felt empowered and privately called my new perspective a "Truth Seeking Mission." In addition to attending our normal weekly church services, I continued leading my small group women's bible study and hoped that doing this one small thing would help me gain new insight on what God had in mind for me. But I told no one in my group of our struggles. Fear and shame kept me silent. The few people who I had worked with in the lay counseling department, who knew what we were going through had promised to pray for us. I knew they tried to understand what we were dealing with but it felt so huge to us that to even begin to imagine talking about it with other people seemed impossible. My own insecurities kept me from reaching out, I felt too needy and I let these thoughts serve as a constant reminder that if people knew what had happened they would turn their backs on us. And so I kept quiet with my small group ladies. I loved them with all my heart, and desperately needed to be a part of the group. To imagine them turning their backs on me was just another burden to bear, so I kept quiet. I needed to be able to focus on something for me, something I knew I was good at. But like anyone who has carried a secret knows, you can't stay in front of it for long, especially when God wants to have it all.

In spite of my stubbornness and naïve expectations, I eventually began to move from the illusions of who I thought God should be and what I thought he should be doing, into a position of acceptance that allowed me to see him with a new perspective. I realized that while I clung to my faith, it really wasn't very deep. My roots had been pulled up and in order for me to find the answers I had to re-plant myself firmly into soil that would be nurtured by God. I surrounded myself with worship music, went to church regularly and facilitated a support network of my closest friends. My prayer was for God to reveal to me who I could trust and who would love us unconditionally through this storm. This small group of close knit friends was handpicked by God, and they never failed to reflect back to me the face and truth of Jesus. I started to see that there would be some things I would never understand and that there was little I could control. I learned that I could take refuge in him, but I had to choose to trust him.

CHAPTER FIVE

Am I Alive in Here?

"There is a loneliness in my spirit, a deep dark chasm that empties nowhere, a hole in my heart that engulfs my senses; a loneliness that is cold."
— *Journal entry*

Grant knew something was wrong before we did the intervention. He had long held the belief that he would die at a young age and imagined on a daily basis how his death would occur. He never told me outright about his feelings until after the intervention and it chilled me to the core how closely his inner thoughts had almost become his reality. I think we both thought this kind of thinking was normal behavior for him, sort of a tortured soul if you will, and we accepted it.

We used to meet for coffee when he had a lunch break and sit and talk about how unhappy he was with his life. He could usually come up with an idea or a dream that would help him pull himself out of the funk. Or he would entertain himself by wandering the aisles in Target, Wal-Mart or Michael's. It seemed a little off to me at the time but he had always been very creative and he told me it made him feel better so I didn't question it.

It wasn't until after the intervention when he began disappearing for hours on end only to call me from a payphone bragging about how many miles he had just walked that I really started to wonder what was driving him. I dismissed my worries as quickly as they came, and didn't pay attention to any kind of cycle, it just seemed like he was prone to mood swings, and sometimes they lasted a few days sometimes they lasted a few weeks. I spent a lot of time trying to figure out what to do and also spent a lot of time desperate to believe that he was going to be okay. I didn't see someone who was mentally ill, I saw someone I had given my heart too. And so I did whatever I could to try and make things better for him and for us.

When you love someone you don't walk away when times get tough, you persevere and hang on to what you know is true. You pull yourself up time and time again hoping that maybe today things will be better, it's how you cope when someone you love is sick. You do whatever you need to do to make things better because if you don't then you might as well be dying right along with them.

Like Jennifer Connelly's character in the movie A Beautiful Mind, I became the steady influence, the one to shoulder the burdens, the ultimate protector and voice of reason. I'll never forget the scene when she realizes something is wrong with her husband. She stands back in horror while she watches him run from window to window urging her to hide, to runaway to her mothers. A frenetic ball of energy he races around the room, mumbling to himself and urges her to hide. "Hurry, Hurry," he cries at her while throwing clothing into a suitcase. "You've got to get out of here, it's not safe." He grabs her and looks her in the eye and pleads with her to not ask any questions, to just, "Please do as I say." Confusion and anger flash across her face as she tries to understand what he is seeing that she cannot. Nothing makes sense to her in that moment except that something is terribly, terribly wrong.

It turns out that he was schizophrenic not bipolar but I saw Grant in him anyway. He saw things through a different filter and despite our struggles I had always gleaned a new insight into the world because of all the ways he shared his knowledge with me. For the first time in our married life I understood just like in the movie, there was no way I was ever going to be able to see through this filter. This was his own private lens, and I was not invited to share it. What I did see was a brilliant man filled with passion, who was now plagued by his own personal demons that no amount of my will could ever exorcise. Here was a brilliant man desperate to live a normal life with absolutely no idea or ability as to how.

In late September we had an argument and ironically something about this reminded me that we were both trying to be alive but not really living. We had fallen into separate routines waiting for something to happen for something to change.

"When is he going to be home?" I voiced my irritation as I glanced at the clock. 10:30pm glared back at me. *Alright, it's not that late yet.* I knew this was a meeting with his co-workers and was glad he had gone. It was a brief respite for me to enjoy my own quiet evening after Zach and Kayla had gone to bed, but I was starting to wonder if waiting up for him had been a good idea.

I channel surfed my way from the news to *Dirty Jobs* and then back to the news. Punching the buttons on the remote, I muttered to myself, "Why do we have so many channels with nothing good to watch?" Tossing the remote aside, I pulled the sheets off and hopped out of bed. *This is a waste of time. I'll just go turn off the lights and go to bed. He's not expecting me to wait up anyway,* I thought grimly. *Why would he?*

As I flipped off the TV I heard the garage door open. I stood very still, holding my breath as I listened to the sounds of keys being dropped on the counter and his wallet slapping the floor as he dropped it. Relief washed over me as I heard him humming a country tune...he sounded good. It was safe.

I wandered quietly down the hall listening to the sounds of cereal being poured into the bowl, milk sloshing over the side. I couldn't help smiling to myself; maybe he really was getting better. Seeing me first, he grinned as milk dribbled down his chin. "Hi, you still up?" His tie hung loosely around his neck, as he shoveled cereal into his mouth. Noticing his jacket folded neatly on the counter, I ran my hands over the soft folds of the material. I loved the way he looked in his suit.

"Yeah, I wanted to see you when you got home." Feeling brave I carefully added, "I missed you." I wrapped my arms around his waist and placed a kiss on his cheek. He kissed me swiftly on the lips, moving away from my embrace. The sweet smell of liquor hung in the air. He had been drinking and didn't want me to know.

Drawing in a deep breath, I decided not to say anything and crawled up on the counter, tucking my knees to my chest and wrapped my arms protectively around them. I held myself tight, bracing for what might be coming next. Alcohol, I knew, dramatically changed him, especially because of his medication. *What was he thinking?*

Anger brewed in the back of my mind as I watched him wash out his cereal bowl. He was like a happy kid after a good day at school. He danced around the kitchen, humming his little tune as he peeled the lid off a bakery cake and prepared to take a giant bite, another indication to me that he had had too much to drink.

He sliced himself a piece of cake, wolfing it down as crumbs canvassed the floor below. He turned and caught me watching him and smiled mischievously. "You know," his voice muffled by the chocolate cake he was trying to swallow, "I have to tell you that my meeting was great, the dinner was great, and I had a really great time." For emphasis he shook his fork at me. He turned his attention back to the cake mumbling, "Man this is good cake. Do you want some?" Holding out the fork to me across the kitchen his eyes met mine and he registered the look of despair that I wore on my face.

"No, I didn't think so. Of course you don't want any."

"Why don't you tell me about your night?" I asked. I hoped with naïveté that making conversation with him would show him that I was more interested than disgusted. But I was disgusted and had been for a very long time.

"Oh, it was fine. We had dinner and then went over to Swigs and had a few drinks. Nothing really, until the guys put me up to a bet." He paused, filling his mouth with more cake.

"Really...what kind of bet?" I asked dreading his response. I knew I was walking into a trap but had no idea how to avoid it.

"Oh, you know...they like to mess with me, and I'm not one to pass up a bet." I nodded so he continued, "There were these two girls, young and pretty, who were sitting across the bar all alone. The guys bet me that I wouldn't go over and talk to them. And you know, I had to laugh because they obviously don't know me and how I am with the ladies." He laughed at no one in particular.

My stomach filled with dread as I asked him, "So what did you do?"

"Well, what do you think I did? Of course I went over there." He glared at me. "I just spent the last two hours hanging out with two beautiful women, talking and laughing. It was fun! I had a great time."

I knew he was waiting for me to react and it took all my resolve to not scream the words that pounded in my head, *Get out! Get out! Get out!* Instead I stayed quiet, afraid if I opened my mouth I would be lost in the storm.

"In fact, I asked them to please explain to me why women are just so weird?" He shook his head, "I don't think I will ever understand you."

I wanted to tear him from limb to limb but managed to keep my cool. I asked in the calmest voice I could muster, "Grant why are you telling me this, did something happen? I don't understand why you are telling me this."

He slammed the cake lid shut and spun around to face me. Staring at me with hateful eyes, he spat in my general direction, "No, nothing happened. But you would love it if something did. Because then you could cart me off to the institution and lock me up, taking all my money, my kids, and my life. Isn't that what you've wanted all along? To lock me up and make me pay?"

His words struck me like a slap on the face, sucking the air out of me. Reeling, I tried to focus on something I knew was true, but all I could think of was him sitting at some bar, pouring his heart out to some strange women. All I had ever wanted was for him to open his heart to me, to share with me who he really was and to let me love him unconditionally. What hurt the most was that he had found that with someone else this night. I had failed him.

My heart was bleeding again, and there was nothing I could do to stop it. I fought against the voices that told me to lash out, to hurt him the way he had hurt me. To remind him that he was the one, who had planned his suicide, planned to leave me and make me pay. But I couldn't, that was not my way.

I willed my frozen legs to move and hopped off the counter to get away from him. I was afraid, and it was time for me to get out of there. "Honey, I love you. We were trying to help you. My parents and Rob, we all love you. No one is trying to hurt you." I knew he wouldn't, couldn't hear me, but I was desperate to convince him.

"Hah, do you really think I believe that!" he wasn't finished yet. "Allison, all I know is that you and your parents are trying to destroy me. And I'm not gonna have it. I'm not going to let you. So you go ahead and call them, have them come down here again and pretend like you want to help me, when in reality you just don't get it. You will never understand me, and I will never understand you. How could you possibly be so selfish?" His last words cut through my shield of defense, and I started to cry.

"Grant, if you tell me that nothing happened tonight, then I believe you. I want us to make this work... we've got to try. Fighting with each other is not going to help us." I pleaded with him as I moved around the counter into the breakfast nook, allowing the half-wall to become a barrier between us. Finding the support I needed, I leaned against the tiled counter waiting for his response.

"Allison," he paused. I imagined him searching his mind carefully for just the right series of words that would put the final stake in my already-devastated heart. His black eyes bore holes into my flesh as I waited for the verdict. I no longer recognized this man. He was lost to me, and in that moment I realized the battle to save his life had truly just begun.

"No, nothing happened. I already said that. I wouldn't be telling you about it if something had."

Relief washed over me as I let out a deflated sigh, "Okay, thank you for telling me the truth. Now can we please stop this arguing and try and look at putting our life back together?"

Angry laughter erupted from his direction as his voice thundered, "Yeah, well, if I thought you weren't going to try and lock me up again, we might actually have a chance." And he walked out of the room.

I wilted against the counter top, my chest heaving, feeling as if I had just battled the enemy head on. I wanted to know when I would feel right again. I wanted to be able to count the days until this horrible sadness would be over. I kept asking God and anyone who would listen, when will this be over? When will my life be better? When will Grant be better? And then gradually I started asking the most relevant question: What comes after grief? I wanted to know so that I could put my hope in something. Anything felt better than where I was.

He was asking himself the same questions only it was worse for him. At least I could escape the constant torment since it didn't live within me, but for Grant there was never any break. He described it like having a constant battle that left him physically and emotionally overwhelmed. He knew his life hung precariously on the edge of a cliff and wondered at what point his illness would send him careening over the edge. He believed God had abandoned him by plaguing him with this horrible illness and wondered like me if his life would ever get any better.

Born out of the paranoia that is part of bipolar came the idea that people were always out to get him. He'd say to me, "Watch out cuz, they're gonna get'cha!" I never knew who "they" were and would just shake my head thinking he was being silly. The truth is he believed it. Never was this truth more obvious then when we were asleep at night. His fears however irrational they might have seemed came alive at night when he was asleep. Since he had spent such a long time in a depressed state his sleep cycles had been interrupted. Starting on the antidepressants was suppose to help him get better, more restful sleep and would induce the active sleep state that produces dreams in most people, but not for Grant. For him sleeping became the worst part of his day. The demons that he was able to consciously avoid during the day came alive at night while he was asleep. He didn't have dreams; he had night terrors of the most terrifying kind. Talking in his sleep came first, then rapid leg movement as if he was running as fast as he could. Followed by a brief lull, then as if re-energized his arms and legs would flail as he screamed at the top of his lungs, "AHHHH!"

Trying to wake someone from a night terror is almost impossible and must be done carefully, especially when they are completely asleep and has pounced on top of you hovering inches from your face growling like a wild animal. After an especially bad night terror happened I started sleeping in the guest room, for my sake as well as his. He never had any memory of what happened during his nightmares, or if he did he never told me.

He was, however, very aware of the things he said to me during the day and how he came across; unfortunately he just didn't care or couldn't care. He was desperately trying to do everything he could to stay above water when all he could think about was how bad he wanted to die. My own anger and self righteousness kept me from seeing how he strategically distanced himself from anyone who might have an idea about what was going on inside his head. In a way he was protecting me from the truth of how bad our situation had become. He knew if he told me how close to the edge he felt I would try and rescue him, and sometimes he just didn't want to be rescued. So instead he was angry and I happened to be the one closest to him, naturally I was the one who bore the brunt of him at his worst. I think on some level that vulnerability was a heavy burden to bear; especially since when he was depressed trusting me or anyone else was almost impossible.

That's the juxtaposition of bipolar...when you're down, you're way down and all you can think about is killing yourself. When Grant was down he said, "It's like torture to be with anyone. Imagine you've got the worst horror movie you've ever seen with the scariest monsters cannibalizing each other because they are fighting over who gets to destroy you." When he was up he wasn't just like superman, he was SUPERMAN and nothing ever got in his way. Every idea was a grand idea, he could do or be anything and nothing could ever hold him back. He says, "Mania is a mind out of control that runs and runs with no way to harness it or draw it in, exhilarating and exciting while energizing all at the same time. It's a world filled with vibrant colors and beautiful music and your mind is putting ideas together in wonderful magical ways."

These were the three men I married, Grant Zero who wanted to kill him, Super Grant who wanted to spend all his money and ruin his life and Normal Grant who had to take responsibility for the damage wrought by the other two. He spent all his time and energy managing this threesome knowing there was no way he could ever rationally explain to someone what it was he was dealing with.

Life was definitely a lot more exciting when Grant was manic but the aftermath was never pleasant and when Grant Zero came on the scene it was like a dark ominous cloud had descended on the entire house sucking the life out of every nook and cranny. Grant Zero was the one who was angry and hurtful, the one who wanted everyone to hurt as much as he did. He was the one who argued with me and blamed me for everything. He was the one I hated the most, not just because of how he treated me but because of how desperate he was to suck the life right out of the real Grant I knew and loved.

Inexplicably he kept his job working on project after project only to fall apart over the weekend. He kept to himself, tried to focus on getting through each day and hoped to convince himself that somehow, by God, he would get through. Months down the road Dr. Peterson called this compartmentalizing. Men are good at this anyway but people like Grant who have a bipolar illness who are high functioning, high achievers are experts in compartmentalizing. They have to be, it's how they survive when all they want to do is put themselves out of their misery.

Grant told me once, "You have no idea how incredibly difficult it is to not listen to that voice in my head that says, *"Just do it, and end it all."* It takes everything in my power to ignore it when all I can think about is how much better off I would be. I wake up every day and hope today is the day I will die." Of course hearing that didn't help me at all. Every time I came home and he was gone my paranoid brain imagined him in a ditch somewhere or parked dead in his car. Or worse, if his car was parked in the driveway and I was coming home I would fear finding him hanging from the ceiling or dead from a gunshot wound to the head.

His ability to compartmentalize helped him tremendously in the early months of his treatment but I didn't understand that it was a survival mechanism, one that helped protect him from himself. It felt to me like I was in the compartment of "Do Not Open" when in reality for him our family compartment was where he sincerely desired to spend the most time because that was where he felt the safest. In spite of the challenges we faced as a couple the compartment where we existed in his head was the place he could let everything down, he could be relaxed and he could rest.

We were trying to be alive, like two soldiers slogging through the swamps of a suffocating battlefield who are surrounded by the stench of death, hoping for a way out focusing our energies on slogging ahead. We were trying to be alive, when it felt like we were both dying inside. But it hadn't always been that way, there had been a time when the love we felt for one another we believed would carry us through life's biggest challenges. New love is like that, vibrant and fresh making you believe anything is possible, making you believe that life is worth living. During the darkest days of Grant's illness I often remembered the first time I heard him say he loved me. These were the words I held close in my heart. These were the words that still made my heart sing.

February 1992 [Longmont, Colorado]

The Rocky Mountains glowed in the distance as the sun dropped, heading to bed for the night. The crisp twilight air caressed me as we walked along, my mitten-covered hand carefully nestled in his. We were on our way to Estes Park and for some reason Grant wanted to stop and go for a walk.

I smiled up at him as he chatted about meeting our

friends at the cabin. The guys, Rob and Sean, were picking up their girlfriends so we could spend the weekend hiking, cooking, and watching movies together. I had just arrived from Washington earlier in the day, and I was not in any hurry to be with anyone else. I wanted to soak up some special time with Grant as it seemed like our weekends together always flew by. It was almost Valentine's Day, and I was thrilled to get to spend it with him.

Shivering against the late winter chill, I moved closer to him as he put his arm around my waist. I laid my head against his shoulder, giggling with delight. There was no place I would rather be.

"Allison, I want you to know something." He stopped walking and turned to face me, taking both my hands in his. I met his gaze and felt a warm blush creep into my cheeks. *What could he be thinking?* I wondered if I should be nervous.

"Allison," he paused again, swallowing. "You know I really care about you, don't you?" I nodded my head as he continued, "I want you to know that…well… it's just that you really mean a lot to me."

I smiled, "Grant you really mean a lot to me too."

Clearing his throat he squeezed my hands tighter and said, "Allison, I'm in love with you. *I love you.*"

Throwing my arms around his neck, I whispered in his ear, "I love you too." He pulled back to look at me. Smiling the sweetest smile I had ever seen, he whispered, "I love you." And then kissed me softly, filling me with a kind of love I had only dreamed of. My heart sang as he picked me up and spun me around shouting over and over again, "I love you, I love you, I love you!" We collapsed into each other's arms, giggling every time. I said, "Say it again! Say it again! Say it again!" I knew I would never grow tired of hearing those three magic words, especially from the man I knew I wanted to spend the rest of my life with.

CHAPTER SIX

It's Not My Fault

"You hem me in-behind and before; you have laid your hand upon me. Such knowledge is too wonderful for me, too lofty for me to attain." Psalm 139:5-6

January 2006

The first six months after we had the intervention were undeniably the worst six months of my life. Trying to navigate without upsetting the delicate balance we had assumed was an ongoing lesson in frustration and anger. We had settled on major depressive disorder as his diagnosis even though I still had questions in my mind about whether he was really bipolar. Typically with new medications improvement begins to happen around six weeks into the regimen and that was true with Grant. But his doctor had warned us that we would not see anything resembling stability for at least six months if not an entire year.

And so my senses ran on overdrive. I never knew what kind of day it would be and my brain had programmed itself to observe any subtle shift in behavior or tone of voice or anything that would indicate danger. Danger that Grant was slipping, danger that we weren't going to make it and danger that I wasn't going to be able to do anything to keep any of it from happening.

During these months I had the same two dreams over and over again. In one dream I would be trying to call him on the phone but could never remember the entire number. Frantic I would call every person I could think of who would know his phone number and each one of them would always respond in the same way, "I don't know his number, Allison, why don't you have it?" Ah, a very good question and it terrified me that I didn't have the answer. In the second dream I was always in the middle of some mundane task like doing laundry or grocery shopping. I would be putting groceries in my grocery cart or laying tee shirts neatly in a pile and notice little drops of blood falling from some part of my body onto the floor. At first I wouldn't be able to find the source of the blood and would go on about my chores ignoring the slow but consistent drip...drip...drip. I would force myself to keep shopping or keep folding laundry until all of a sudden the slow drip would change into a bleeding river of blood. In horror I would grab anything that would quench the flow but the blood just kept pouring right from the middle of my stomach its source the very deepest part of my soul. By then it was always too late and I knew in the dream that I was dying.

By the time I woke up screaming from these nightmares, I was always convinced that Grant was truly dead. They say that when you're asleep your unconscious mind takes over. Apparently my unconscious mind was acting out the fears I could not comprehend in my waking hours. Comfort came however; as I reached out to him after every dream and placed my hand on his back or arm. Feeling the warmth of his skin beneath my fingers reassured me. He was still filled with the warmth of life and not the stone cold sensation of death. I was the one dying a little every day, losing myself in the midst of the seemingly endless months we spent waiting to see if he was going to get better. I was the one dying a slow painful death. Never was this more evident than when our trying to do normal things collided with the obvious truth that something was very very wrong in our life. Like the day when we were getting ready to have friends in for the Rose Bowl. That was the day when I hit a crepe myrtle and an orange post spoke volumes to me about how crazy our life had become.

"Honey," I shouted up the stairs hoping Grant would hear me the first time. We only had about thirty minutes before our friends were going to arrive to watch the Rose Bowl, which meant I had to hurry. "Honey!" I called again, this time with a little more urgency. "I'm going to pick up Kayla, I'll be right back. Can you hear me?"

Grant's voice echoed down the stairwell, "Yes, fine. I'll be hitting the shower in a minute."

I turned from the stairwell and hustled back to the kitchen grabbing my keys and purse on the way. I was excited about having our friends over to watch the game and even though we weren't really huge fans of the Texas Longhorns it would be a fun game to watch. As I backed my Sequoia out of the garage I remembered that I had bumped one of the Crepe Myrtle trees earlier that day. It seemed like I was always bumping them a little but this time one of the branches was broken and I knew he wasn't going to be happy. He had argued against planting the trees the previous summer for exactly this reason. His words ran across my brain as I pulled out of the driveway. "I know what will happen; I know you will back into them. There is no point in planting them along the driveway. They'll just get wrecked." After I promised to be extra careful he finally relented and had planted six beautiful trees that were now dormant for the winter. I was going to have to do some heavy duty explaining when I got home.

Kayla hopped in the car and chattered about her friends, how much fun she had with them and wondered out loud "Mom, why did I have to come home so soon?" I glanced at her in the rearview mirror. Her freckled cheeks glowed with excitement as she told me about her day. She always amused me with her animated gestures and bubbly little voice. "Well honey, we've got some friends coming over tonight. Do you remember?" I looked back at her again, her eyes met mine. I could see her question before she asked it and so I quickly interjected, "Yes, honey some of your friends too." She smiled back at me and proceeded to talk in general, not really caring if I responded. She was content in her own little world. I pulled the car into the driveway her sweet voice echoing through my mind as I mentally checked off the tasks that still needed to be finished before our friends arrived.

I reached up to click the garage door opener and saw out of the corner of my eye an orange post hammered into the ground. What in the world could that be and, why was it hammered into the ground, in the exact spot where the tree with the broken branch used to be? I parked the car in the garage and silently walked out into the driveway. The tree had been chopped to the root. Viciously hammered into the splintered stump was the orange post. Chilled by the early evening breeze, I wrapped my arms around myself trying to control the undeniable urge I had to scream. I closed my eyes, wishing I could wipe away the image that had been indelibly placed in my brain. I wondered how long this beacon would scream recriminations at me. How long would I be forced to endure these kinds of random actions of hate that he continued to heave in my direction? Was there nothing that I could do right? The post might as well have been hammered directly into my heart since I couldn't breathe. Tears began to trickle down my cheeks as I wished I could be anyplace else. I really wished he was dead.

Kayla came up behind me and gently placed her hand in mine quietly asking,

"Mom, why is there an orange post where the tree used to be?"

I wiped the tears from my cheeks, squeezed her hand to offer reassurance and squatted down so I could look her straight in the eye. "Honey, I think Daddy must have put it there but I'm not sure why. Let's not worry about it right now, okay?" No matter how much pain I was in, she could not know and so I willed myself to speak calmly, hoping that her memory would be wiped clean of this event. She smiled at me and nodded her head before she bounced through the garage door into the kitchen.

I walked over to the orange post. Somehow Grant had discovered the broken branch on his own. I ran my hands over the orange paint, the wood splintered into my fingertips but I was immune to the pain. A much deeper gnawing had opened itself up inside me. This was his way of telling me I was a disappointment, and I had failed.

I wrapped my hands around the post impervious to the piercing of my flesh as I tugged and tugged. Desperate to yank the post out I tried and tried but finally had to step back exhausted by the effort. There was no way I was going to get the post out. I fought back more tears of frustration as I climbed back into the driver's seat of my car. I felt my own personal cloak of shame fall heavily onto my already burdened shoulders. Gone was the excitement I felt about having our friends come over. I dialed my Mom.

"Hello?" The sound of her voice broke through the barrier I had placed around my heart. Words escaped me as I sobbed into the phone. I heaved and cried, managing to form a few intelligible words along the way. "Mom...it's uh...it's me, Allison." The silence across the phone line was punctuated with the sound of my sobs. She didn't ask and she didn't probe, she just waited. I started to scream into the phone.

"Mom, I don't know how much more of this I can take! He's making me crazy! I have no idea what I'm supposed to do, this isn't the life I wanted and all I did was break a stupid tree branch. He's totally freaking out, chopped the tree down and now I've got people coming over and everyone is going to know!" I paused to catch my breath and she quickly interrupted me asking, "Honey, what is everybody going to know?"

"Everyone is going to know that I'm a failure. How am I supposed to pretend that everything is okay when it's not? How come he does these things and makes me feel like it's all my fault? I didn't mean to break the tree branch Mom, it was an accident."

"Yes, honey, I know. But why would everyone think you were a failure? You've hung in there; you've done everything you could to work with this awful situation. If he's mad about the tree, let him be mad about the tree."

"But Mom, what am I supposed to do? I was so excited about having our friends over, it made me feel like we were making progress. Now all I can think about is how mad I am at him, and how much I wish I was anyplace but here. How am I supposed to pretend that everything is okay, Mom? All I can think about right now is how much easier my life would be right now if he really had died. And I feel so guilty for feeling that way!" A fresh crop of tears broke through and I began wailing inconsolably into the phone.

My mom's stern voice burst through the sounds of

my sobs, "Oh, Allison. I know you don't really wish he was dead. That's just your pain talking right now. Honey, he's still getting better, I know it's hard to remember that. We all wish he was better right now." I nodded in agreement through my tears as I listened to her, wishing she could hug me.

"Allison, you have to make a choice. You can sit here and keep crying or you can call it what it is. You've got to get a focus on what you know is true. You know breaking the tree branch was an accident. You know that what he did was unacceptable. You can still have your party and just blow this off." Her words soothed me. We talked for a little bit longer and then I hung up the phone. She was right, I was going to have this party and not let the orange post taunt me any longer.

With renewed focus I walked into the house with my mom's words floating around in my head. I told myself that I wasn't going to feel shame about breaking the tree branch. I knew it was an accident and I knew that my intentions were good. I was going to ask him to get the post out of the yard before our friends came over. I was hoping we could both save face and then talk it out after everyone left, talk about naïve expectations.

I followed the sounds of water flowing from the shower in our bathroom. He was just stepping out of the shower as I came in. He was such a handsome man, even after all these years just looking at him could make my heart sing. My heart caught in my throat as I realized how much I loved him and how desperately I wanted to make things right. I stood quietly in the doorway waiting to see if he would speak first. After a few minutes passed he finally cleared his throat, "Um, hmm? Did you have something you wanted to say to me?" His tone suggested he knew exactly why I was in the bathroom so I took the invitation and blurted out, "Honey, I broke the tree branch. I'm sorry, it was an accident and I know you're upset about it. I wish it hadn't happened, I'm just really sorry." I waited for him to accept my apology but none came.

I continued, "I was in a hurry and I guess I wasn't paying attention. But I don't understand why you chopped the tree down. Can you please explain that? And what is the deal with that orange post? Is that supposed to be some kind of joke, because if it is I don't think it's very funny. In fact I find it hurtful and mean. I would like you to take it out before our friends get here." Encouraged by my words I allowed myself to look him straight in the eye as I made my last request and immediately recoiled at the venomous look he shot at me.

I took a step backwards wondering what kind of ammunition was about to be unleashed when he threw his towel down and slammed his fist on the countertop.

"I'll tell you what the post is for," he snarled. "That's the freaking post so that my freaking wife won't run down the freaking trees anymore because she's too freaking blind to watch out for the freaking tree. So, now you get a freaking orange post! Maybe that will remind you to be a lit-tle more care-ful!" He sneered at me placing extra emphasis on the last three words and then marched away from me into our closet.

Stunned by his anger, although I'm not sure what it was I expected, I stood there for a brief moment and then made a decision. If he wasn't going to take the post out of the yard I wasn't going to give it another thought. I had moved from feeling bereft and forlorn to empowered and angry. If anyone of our friends asked about the post I would just casually brush it off and say something like, "Oh, well, you know that's just a little reminder for me to be careful about the trees." And then I would smile sweetly, knowing they wouldn't press it. Even though I was seething inside I was an expert at keeping my true emotions hidden. I could keep pretending, it was second nature to me now, just like when I was a little girl.

As a girl my favorite toy was my Barbie, or should I say Barbies? I had mountains of them, piles and piles of Barbie clothing, several cars, and several Ken dolls with different plastic hair color. I could have made millions in Barbie real estate with enough equipment to build many Barbie houses. I could play for hours, setting up a Barbie city in the basement of my home, thankfully my Mom didn't mind and so I could keep things set up for days, sometimes even weeks. The game was always the same, fix Barbie's hair, pick out a pretty dress and get her ready for her date. She was always beautiful, always perfect and always, always had just the right thing to say. She was beautiful to everyone, especially to Ken. He never stood her up, never ignored her or forgot her birthday and never, ever told her it was awful to have her for a wife. He loved her, drove her to nice restaurants, talked kindly to her, promised to slay dragons for her and always made her feel like a princess, and she believed him. What Barbie didn't count on was in every story there is a villain, sure she had Ken to protect her but what would Barbie do if the person she loved with every part of her heart became the very thing she was most afraid of? Then what would Barbie do?

My real life fairy tale began the night of December 21, 1992 when Grant asked me to marry him. He had been the prince in my story, or the Ken to my Barbie for a very long time. He was the first person I had called when I became a Christian. He was the one I had spent hours on the phone with giggling and laughing throughout high school. He was the one that in spite of all my insecurities, made me feel secure. I had loved him for as long as I could remember and had only dreamed of a future with him. After two and a half years of long distance dating my dream of becoming his wife was finally coming true.

The night he proposed we escaped to a romantic Italian dinner which was no small feat. He was only going to be home from the Air Force Academy for a few days, normally that meant we spent all of his time with his family. I was just glad to be with him at all.

We stood in the middle of a snow covered frozen river bed just beyond the Sunriver Lodge in central Oregon. He sank onto one knee burying his leg in a snowdrift, while reaching out to take my hand. Smiling he spoke the words I had heard only in my dreams. "Allison Rouse, will you marry me?"

Too stunned for words, I had to find my voice. On the third try I shouted with glee, "Yes, yes, I will marry you!" He quickly tore my gloves off and placed a sparkling diamond onto my finger. "You have made me the happiest girl in the world," I shouted as I dove into his arms kissing him all over the face. Tears of joy flowed freely down my cheeks as he pulled himself away taking my face in the palms of his hands. He smiled at me breathlessly and kissed the tip of my nose, "No Allison...you have made me the happiest man in the world." And then his lips pressed down on mine sealing this precious moment forever. We were going to be married, we were going to live our own fairy tale and we would be happy.

What I hadn't anticipated was how devastated he would be when I told him the truth about my past. I had kept the secret for so long it was only now since we were safely engaged that I knew I could share with him the most painful part of my life. I wanted to believe he would understand and love me no matter what, but the voice of doubt grew in my mind over the following weeks until I couldn't stand it anymore and I finally told him.

"Grant, there is something I need to tell you." I whispered softly to him as we sat together enjoying the moonlit Colorado sky. It had been almost two months since our engagement and I had flown to Colorado for a long weekend to be with him. I knew what I was about to tell him would break his heart but I also knew that if I didn't share my whole story with him, there was no way I could marry him.

He smiled at me from across the hot tub, "Well, okay…what is it." He reached out and caressed the side of my cheek, moving forward to kiss me. I moved my face away and wrapped my arms around his neck instead. The night sky glistened as the stars beckoned to me. I imagined each star as an angel calling my name, encouraging me to take responsibility for my part and at the same time I understood that as I shared this burden it would no longer be only mine to bear. I needed him to understand and know all of me. I needed him to accept me; I couldn't stand any longer to wonder if he would still love me if he knew the truth and so I told him.

"Grant, I'm not a virgin, I was sexually abused as a small child and since then I've been involved with a lot of other men." The muscles in his back stiffened as the truth of my words pierced him. He jumped back throwing water over the edge of the hot tub, astonishment crept across his face, then shock and then finally anger.

"What in the world are you talking about? I don't understand why you're telling me this now?" He looked confused for a moment and then continued, "Allison, why didn't you tell me this before? You've been lying to me all along?" His voice cracked at the last part and I choked on my words desperate for him to understand the depth of the shame and horror that I felt.

"I think you've known for awhile that I wasn't a

virgin, in fact you told me that you knew that. But what you didn't know is why I have been the way I've been. Now you know that there was more to the story, now you know that somewhere along the line I was abused and used by many men." I gulped back my tears determined to get past the ugliness in my mind, hoping that our love would be strong enough to handle this revelation.

"Well, yeah, guys used to talk about you in the locker room, but I never wanted to believe it." He stared blankly at me as he mentally recounted the locker room scenes in his mind. I shuddered to think of the kinds of things that had been said about me, knowing I could never go back and change the things I had done. What I did know was the abuse wasn't my fault but I had made terrible choices, and allowed myself to do things that I had never wanted to admit to anyone until now. I waited, crying out to God in my mind to take care of this situation. Grant closed his eyes and sank back against the wall of the hot tub. He seemed to relax and I hoped he was going to say something that would make me believe everything was going to be okay.

Instead, his eyes flew open, as he grabbed one fist with the other. He was enraged now; I could see it in his eyes. And then I knew this was the end. "How'd you get so good with those knives Allison? Because right now you've just stabbed me in the back and I'm finished with you."

He stood up, wrapped a towel around his waist and walked towards the house. "Grant, wait, please." I tried to catch up with him but he had already gone into the bathroom to change. I sank onto the edge of the couch and quietly began praying to myself. My body shook with fear, what if I had done the wrong thing? What if this was the breaking point and he didn't want to have anything to do with me? What if this really was the end? I had to believe we would get through. The Lord had been speaking to me for weeks about telling him the truth. Even though I knew telling him would hurt him, I had decided it was the only way.

I handed him my engagement ring when he sank onto the couch next to me. With tears streaming down my face I knew in my heart this was the right thing to do. I wanted to believe I was good enough for him but I knew that I never would be. Here was this perfect Christian guy who had been raised in the church, who had succeeded so far in everything he had attempted and who had held onto the hope that the woman he married would be as clean and pure as he was. But I was damaged and dirty, believing that nothing could ever wash that stain away. His words confirmed my fears as he took my hand in his. "Allison, I can't marry you."

Silently I shook my head and then pleaded with him. "Please try and understand, I never meant to hurt you. I didn't tell you about all of this because I was afraid. You know I'm not a bad person...it's just; well I just hate that part of my life. I'm so sorry Grant, please forgive me. Please forgive me."

For the rest of the night we alternately prayed and cried and then prayed some more. By the time the sun was rising over the Black Forest we were engaged again, but it would take ten years before we were finally able to put the shame of my past behind us.

For years I believed that if only I could be good enough, pretty enough, smart enough...the list could go on and on. My childhood sexual abuse was the root of significant self esteem issues for me that caused daily struggles in my relationship with Grant. I was haunted by the sins of my past wondering every single day when he would change his mind and leave. In the early days of his illness I thought his violent mood swings were because of me, that if he had never married me then maybe he would have been happy. I thought about leaving him to give him the chance at a better life but I was afraid and honestly hoped somehow we would work things out. Like any other abuse survivor I believed I was lucky to have someone who seemed to love me part of the time.

His behavior after the intervention made sense to me. He was angry and I was the cause of his anger. On some level I thought it was exactly what I deserved. What I didn't understand was my self esteem issues were totally unrelated to what was happening inside of him. After the intervention it would take almost two years before we finally heard the words, "He's actually a bipolar patient."

Treating a bipolar patient with antidepressants is like putting a band-aid on a person who has a cancerous mole. It might make them feel better for awhile but in fact is not doing anything to help the situation; it actually makes things worse by giving the patient and their families a false sense of hope and can actually bring on manic episodes. The patients continue to get sicker; their illnesses grow out of control and for the bipolar patient the risk of suicide increases exponentially. That was the reason why things continued to get worse. Since depression is far more common than bipolar disorder, often early treatment has to rule out depression before moving to a diagnosis of bipolar. Therefore, it's critical that the patient stay in close contact with their doctor. Only through the diligent care of a qualified doctor and a strong commitment from the patient to stay in treatment can you ultimately get to the right diagnosis.

CHAPTER SEVEN

Turning Inward

"The search for God and the search for self are greatly intertwined." —Jerome Daley

I felt crazy and exhausted all the time. Denial takes a toll on you no matter what sorts of stories you tell yourself. It's what you deny that eats away at your soul. Denial was my way of coping with our situation and I actually believed that things were getting better. Never mind that I had cut myself off from a lot of my friends, socializing was too exhausting. Never mind that my normal way of being was to be with people, to have fun and enjoy whatever adventure popped up. Never mind that I pasted a smile on my face on a daily basis hoping that if I smiled all the time, maybe somehow I would actually feel like smiling.

My focus was surviving from one day to the next, protecting Zach and Kayla from whatever their dad might do or say. I focused on being normal and doing normal things. Because doing normal made me feel normal. And I so desperately wanted to be normal. Normal is good and pleasant and makes me feel better. Being normal on the outside made me believe that I was normal on the inside. What's funny to me now is how far from normal we were and how anyone with half a brain could have seen that. I don't include myself in that category since it is very obvious that if I had half a brain, I probably could have seen and called it what it was, DENIAL. Instead I might as well have had a bullhorn in my hand and shouted to anyone within earshot, "Keep moving, there's nothing to see here!" That would have been a little more subtle.

I wished I held a bullhorn in my hands so that I could yell for help, as I sat on the edge of the rock paralyzed, frozen with fear. My ragged breath tore at the tightness in my chest. The sun beat down on my head, and the wind whipped my hair around my face, catching the tears that were brimming, and ready to spill down my cheeks. I was stuck, I needed help. "Mommy, are you scared?" Kayla, my daughter, looked over at me. She was sitting next to me on the same rock, and I wondered if I should tell her the truth, or tell a bold face lie. "Yes, darlin', I'm scared, but we will get down from here I promise."

"Ok," she replied, innocently placing her trust in me. She sat down and waited for me to decide what to do.

It was New Year's Eve. The weather was perfect for a Texas winter day spent hiking up Enchanted Rock. It's not a difficult climb, and something we, Grant and I, had talked about doing for a long time. We had heard from other families with young children that it was an easy climb, and something our eight and nine year old children should be able to do with no problem. We were excited to picnic first, and then make the one mile climb up the face of the rock. Given the terrain, smooth, and without steep incline, we got to the top quickly. The kids seemed to enjoy the crisp winter air, and chased each other around the top, darting in and out of rock formations, screaming with glee when one caught the other. It was such a beautiful spot, and I enjoyed gazing out at the rolling Texas hills, dotted with still green live oak trees.

Feeling adventurous, we decided to make our descent down on a different trail. As we progressed down the rock face, I quickly realized that my shoes were not easily tracking the smooth rock surface, as they had on the climb up. It didn't help that I was wearing my oldest tennis shoes; of course they didn't have any traction. The rock face was slick, and much steeper on this new trail. I tried to follow Grants lead, and step where he stepped, but I rapidly fell behind, Kayla did as well.

By the time I found myself sitting on the edge of the rock, I was ready to quit. Ready for someone to fly in, scoop me up and settle me safely at the bottom of the hill. My head was shouting self recriminations, "What are you doing here?" "You know you can't do this!" "What are you thinking? There is no way you are going to make it down this rock that now feels like a giant mountain!" My heart was racing, gripping me with fear. Not just fear for my own safety, but fear for my children as well. I could see them and myself in my mind's eye tumbling down the face of the rock, landing broken and lifeless at the bottom. *No, I don't think I really believe that we are going to get down.* And so I sat there, my daughter on one side of me, my husband and son farther down the hill, looking back with wonder and curiosity at the two of us perched on the edge of the rock face.

"Mom?" Kayla's voice broke into the tornado of anxious thoughts flying around my head. "Mom, what are we going to do?" I looked over at her, wishing I had the answer and then hiding my panic calmly called down the rock face to Grant and Zach who were about 100 yards below.

"Grant," I called out to him. "I need you to come up here and help me." He just stared back at me. I knew he could hear me but why wasn't he answering me?

As calmly as I could I tried again, only with a little more conviction this time, "Honey, I need you to come and get Kayla, our shoes are too slippery and I'm afraid we are going to fall down the face of this rock." I used to pretend to be someone else when I was a kid, now all I wanted was for him to be someone else. I wanted him to be the sweet person I married, I needed that person to come and help me but I was starting to see less and less of that man and more and more of the darkness that was taking him over.

Nothing… no response, he didn't move an inch and continued to stare blankly at me. "Grant…" He interrupted me, irritated, "I heard you, Allison, but there is nothing I can do for you. It's not my fault you wore the wrong shoes. There is no place for you to go, except down. So, you'll just have to figure it out." He stood there, blinking up at me. His words washed over me, but I didn't want to believe them.

"Hey, Mom, I can help you!" Zach began climbing back up the mountain. Oh, that sweet boy. The dam holding my tears almost broke, but I refused to melt, especially since it was obvious my children were very tuned in to what was going on. What else were they seeing that I wasn't aware of?

"Zach, it's ok, I want you to stay down there." My heart broke. The truth in that moment spoke volumes to me; I was alone, not worthy of his help and more of an inconvenience to him than ever. How dare I wear the wrong shoes? It was my own fault, and I should have planned better. I felt ashamed of my weakness and ashamed that my own children had seen me in this state of anxiousness. I had to figure out how to get myself down, and safely, with Kayla in tow.

I sucked up the urge to cry, scream and shout obscenities, and instead began talking myself out of my panic attack. I began directing Kayla down, by having her scoot on her bottom, I followed directly behind her. Grant held out his arms, connecting himself with a tree branch, and caught Kayla. He did the same for me.

Several days later Grant and I sat in our counselor's office relating the tale of what happened on Enchanted Rock. "Why wouldn't you come up there and help me," I asked Grant. He looked at me incredulously, and responded to the counselor, "It would never have occurred to me to help her, not in a million years, that's just ridiculous."

That was his answer at that moment on that day,

but if you asked him the same question a week or a month later there was no guarantee he would answer the same way. His moods were so unpredictable, that I thought for sure I was losing my mind. Of course I read my Bible, prayed and tried to stay focused on our mission of getting him better but the constant changes in his behavior, the seemingly endless list of reasons why it was always my fault and the deep sadness I felt caused me to guard my heart at all costs. There was a giant disparity from day to day of what he would and would not do for me. I was waiting for him to rescue me never thinking that I could participate in rescuing myself.

When I was small my sisters and I built forts out of couch cushions. We would angle them just right so they would keep each other up. My sisters and I would drape a blanket over the top for a roof and haul all kinds of stuff inside pretending that we were stranded in a blizzard back in the olden days or that we were hiding from wild animals in a dark, foreboding cave. When night fell that made it even more fun because we could take flashlights into our fort and pretend the power had gone out, giggling with glee we would create another imaginary scene where we needed rescue of some sort. We always needed rescuing and we were happy to wait. Someone would always come and take care of us rescuing us from the imaginary danger we had created. We were selective in who we let in and fought passionately to keep anyone else out. It was exhilarating to be the chief Indian fighting against the settlers, or to be the princess needing help or the vicious dragon that was locked out. The fort was a magical place where we could be strong or vulnerable, excited or scared. It was our place of refuge that allowed us to exorcise our own fears and dreams. But maybe it was more than that; maybe it was a place for us to hide from the terror in our own hearts.

It was sad when we had to put the fortress away. Our enchantment disappeared as we placed the blankets back in the closet and settled couch cushions back into their spots. There was something about turning inward and digging up the images from my own imagination that made me feel free. I could be strong within the realm of my fortress; I could slay my own dragons, fight my own battles or just hide. From behind the wall of couch cushions I could be anyone I wanted to be and it was magic. But a man made fortress never survives; eventually it will sustain a blow so devastating that the walls tumble trapping its occupants inside. Only the fortress and refuge that Jesus provides in Psalms 91 is truly impenetrable. There is nothing the world can launch at us if we take refuge in Him. By dwelling in the shelter of the Most High we are covered, we are protected and have no reason to fear. We are told that, "Because he loves me, I will rescue him; I will protect him, for he acknowledges my name." Jesus promises to answer us when we call upon His name, he promises to deliver us and give us rest.

I heard a story once about a woman who loved Psalm 91. She was fascinated by the idea that God was not only a shelter in times of trouble but actually a refuge, a safe place to rest. She loved the analogy of verse 4, "He will cover you with feathers and under his wings you will find refuge." She told her son the story about how God promises to be our refuge in times of trouble and how we can rest beneath the shadow of his wings like a baby bird does under its mothers. She explained to her five year old son that God is like a fortress that we can run into and find ourselves safe from the outside world or any enemy that might be trying to harm us. Satisfied with her description she wondered what her son was thinking. She sat quietly next to him, knowing he was thinking about the story and waited for him to put his thoughts into words. Thoughtfully he turned and placed both hands against her cheeks so that he knew she would not turn away. In a very serious voice he said, "Mom, you know the fortress isn't only where we get our protection," he paused and then with a mischievous smile he said, "It's also where we can turn around and fight."

Believe me, I was fighting, every single day, but not from the fortress God had built for me, I was fighting a losing battle from the bowels of my own fortified castle of shame when I could have been standing within the walls of a mighty castle surrounded by legions of angels whose only desire was to give me exactly what I needed. Unfortunately I had built the walls so high and so deep I began to fear there would be no way God or anyone else would ever hear my anguished cries for help. I called and called to God from the deepest part of my fortress, "Oh God, please help me, please rescue me from this madness! Please help me Lord, I'm lost and I just don't know what to do." I waited, desperate for deliverance and wondered when God would rescue me.

You see, the Lord will not save a person against his will but He has a thousand ways of making his heart more willing. I didn't understand that at the time but now I know that in order to be saved or rescued by God I had to be willing to leave my own self made place of refuge. Only once I abandoned my own strength would I be able to walk directly into the place of refuge God had built for me. Not an easy thing to do, especially since my own hideout felt so safe and warm. We all do it; we are blinded to the squalor that surrounds our man made shelters and wonder why everyone else seems so much better off. We wonder why we can't live like they do but can't bring ourselves to leave what we know to be familiar and safe. And we'll take familiar and safe even if it means unpleasant and dirty because familiar and safe make us feel like we haven't lost all control. Familiar and safe are good for those of us who have no idea what to do, so we choose to do nothing but continue to hide.

I thought I lived in a castle built on strength and power, and prided myself in my ability to protect myself. In reality if I had stepped outside of the castle and had God's perspective on where I was I would have seen a lamely built, rickety, moldy little shanty of shame that could have been knocked down with one mighty gust of wind. The foundation was eroded by anger and bitterness, the walls crawled with plagues and pestilence and the roof sagged beneath the weight of despair and darkness. I lived in my own little shanty of shame and sitting there on the edge of that rock showed me I was finally ready to knock it down. I had been asking, seeking, knocking for such a long time that I almost missed the door opening.

At some point we have to stop asking everyone else to help us and ask ourselves, "How can I help myself?" My friends, my family, my counselor all provided me with their own ideas and input about what they thought I should or shouldn't do. Ultimately I knew the decision was mine, I had to choose, was I going to continue living in the contemptible shame shanty that left me weary and afraid, or was I going to take that step of faith I knew I had to take and finally trust God to receive me into his wings of protection?

Maybe it was the lack of rescue that did it, or that moment in time that I realized there was no way I was going to get what I needed from Grant, he was still sick and could be sick for a very long time. I had to dig deep inside myself to find my own way down the rock face. Or maybe it was God giving me the ability to see how paralyzed I was hiding inside my shanty of shame, how deeply buried I was beneath the rubble that Grant's illness had caused. Or maybe my quest for truth was finally coming to an end. Something had shifted inside my house of shame and there was no way I could deny any longer the equipment and skills God had been launching over the walls I had built. He had been equipping me all along, but I had been looking away from the truth that was in my heart.

Like I said earlier, denial is what erodes your soul

making you believe lies, and fabricates stories you would much rather believe. It's only when we are willing to look into our hearts, into our wounds allowing Christ to fortify and build us up that we will be able to embrace our destiny and answer the call of where He is leading us. It's when we don't pay attention to where God is leading us that we get off track. And amazing how quickly we assume that when something bad happens we must be off track. What if the trauma and tragedy are actually part of the road to our destiny? What if the bad choices we make or the shame we feel about them are actually part of what God intended to help us get to where He wants us to be? If we knew this without any doubt wouldn't we then stomp out every seed of untruth and run as fast as we could right into his arms?

In Isaiah 61, "He has sent me to bind up the brokenhearted, to proclaim freedom for the captives and release from darkness for the prisoners." He binds us up, releases us from captivity and shines His light on those things we keep hidden. But He also gave us free will, so we have to choose to come out of our chaos and darkness and allow Him to keep us on track. If we want healing we have to let Him in, to touch those parts in us we wish we could ignore. George MacDonald prayed, "Gather my broken fragments to a whole . . . Let mine be a merry, all-receiving heart, but make it a whole, with light in every part." But we can't do this alone. If we really want our hearts to be whole, we have to allow Jesus to bind up our broken hearts, we have to be willing to let him in to our darkness and we have to go there with Him, allowing him to show us what we didn't want to see.

Sitting there on the edge of that rock in spite of my fear and anxiety I saw the sorry state of my family. I saw the faces of my children staring at me with curiosity, trying to figure out how they could help me. I saw the distorted face of my husband who I no longer recognized challenging me to fail. And I saw God standing next to Grant on the hillside, with a smile on his face, his arms crossed against his chest, waiting patiently for me to get past myself and jump into his arms letting him carry me from my shame shanty into the fortified place of refuge he was ready to provide.

Contrary to everything I had ever been taught about being a Christian woman and acting with respect and reverence to my mate, was the idea that I could indeed take matters into my own hands and fight for myself, for my own survival. To take matters into my own hands seemed to smack of disrespect not only to my husband but also to my God. But, desperate times call for desperate measures…especially when you find yourself caught in a losing battle that you haven't been willing to fight.

It was time for me to fight for myself and for my children. This was no time to wait for rescue, no time for whining and crying. I had to snap out of it, stop being a victim, use my head and stand up and fight. Fight for myself, my children and my family. It was time to listen to my support network that had been telling me for months to "be prepared for anything" and "to use my instincts," running if I had to. God had already equipped me to handle some pretty terrible situations, so why would he stop equipping me now?

After almost two years I had finally come to the crossroads I had been hoping to avoid. I knew that if I stood up and started to fight for myself and my family there was a very real possibility that Grant would become my enemy. Not the Grant I knew and loved but the monster that had taken him over. There was no way to separate the two; they shared the same body…which meant I would have to fight the man I loved.

The decision was made for me; I can't explain it any other way. After sitting in Robert's office for the second counseling session in as many weeks, I heard Grant say he didn't have any idea where we were going or what we were doing. When I heard him say, "I don't know what we are doing, there's no way I can tell you that anything is any better," I stood up, threw my notebook onto Robert's desk and howled, angry hollow sobs wracking my body. *This again, I thought we had gotten past this? No! I am not going down this path again, I can't!*

Somehow my tears dried up and I slowly turned around and looked at Robert, who was staring intently at Grant who was staring directly at me. Confusion colored his green eyes, creating clouds of doubt that he quickly covered by cracking a joke. This was nothing new to me and yet Grant seemed to think I had never heard him express his doubts about our future. I had heard the same thing off and on for months. One week we were the best couple ever, the next week he was leaving me for a better life. It was a roller coaster ride I could never get off of, until now. I had had enough. I was done.

I sank onto the edge of the couch shoving my angry emotions back inside my heart. My mind wandered as Robert and Grant discussed a few random things to finish up the appointment. I couldn't stop thinking about all the times people had said to me that I needed to prepare myself for anything. I had fought them, "No way," I would say, "It's going to be okay." But in my darkest moments I couldn't deny that I was looking for a way out. I was tired of waiting for rescue, and even more tired of the ridiculous roller coaster ride we were on. Even the nurse from the psychiatrist's office had said to me several times, "Mrs. Johnson the best thing you can do is take care of yourself and your children. You need to do whatever it takes to protect yourself."

Of course I always smiled at her words thinking she didn't have a clue what she was talking about but now I knew she was exactly right. Chills ran up my neck as I began formulating a plan in my mind. It was time for me to rescue myself and my children; it was a matter of life and death, only this time the people hanging by a thread were one scared mom and two innocent children. I would have to do whatever it took to protect myself and Zach and Kayla, it was the only way we would survive. I felt a new energy and sense of direction. There were going to be some new rules of engagement and I was going to make them.

Stepping out into the sunlight from the office building I was blinded by extremely bright noon day sun. Squinting against the glare I moved across the parking lot my fingers searching for the jumble of keys I had thrown into my purse earlier. I waved at Grant as I opened the door of my silver Sequoia and then sank into the drivers' seat dropping my head against the steering wheel. I closed my eyes as I turned the key in the ignition, allowing the blast of air conditioning to beat against my face. I felt myself drift away from the parking lot and allowed my imagination to take over.

Instead of sitting in a parking lot in the heat of the Texas noonday sun I found myself standing right in the middle of a giant coliseum, surrounded by legions of angels who had their swords drawn. From inside the coliseum the sounds of the outside world were quieted by the gentle hum of the angels' voices as they murmured their approval and welcomed me with smiles and silent nods. Looking around I could see the doors were fortified with several layers of solid oak, and the windows so transparent they almost seemed invisible. But the light was what consumed me, filling me so completely I felt my chest swell with joy. I closed my eyes for a moment drinking in this place, this oasis in my desert, this place that I had longed for but never seen. I wanted to sing and dance and laugh and twirl! And so I did, running from window to window, giggling with delight. I smiled to the angels, nodded to the warriors and sang and sang and sang.

And then a mirror appeared in the middle of the enormous coliseum. At first I hesitated, my joy replaced with curiosity tinged with fear. I walked towards the mirror my eyes searching for my reflection but there was nothing there. I glanced around the coliseum, what was this place? Where was I? I searched the crowd of angels hoping for answers, finding none; I stared back at the mirror. Silence filled the coliseum, as gloom consumed the glorious light, shrinking it until it was contained by the framework of the giant mirror. I looked deeper into the mirror the light piercing my eyes, reflecting back to me a person I did not recognize. I was covered in filth, seeing myself for the first time, through my uncovered eyes. Anguished sobs wracked my body as I sank to my knees weeping at the sight. I knew if I wanted to stay in this place of heavens light, I had to allow the glorious light to reappear. I was the reason the coliseum had gone dark, and the light only came from the mirror placing a spotlight on my sin and shame. I was the reason the light had gone away and I was desperate to get it back again.

For the first time I knew where I was. I stood within the walls of a giant sanctuary built especially for me. It was my own place of refuge, my own coliseum fortified by legions of angels who were my allies, warriors who would fight with me and for me. This new place was far better than anything I could ever have imagined and I wanted to stay.

I stood up quietly and looked deeply into the mirror, repulsed by the vision I saw, I cried out to God, "Oh Lord, I need you, I need you, I…need…you! Please wash me with your blood, make me whole, make me clean…have mercy upon me and forgive me Lord for not trusting in you."

The light poured from the mirror, piercing my flesh sending the plagues and pestilence I had carried scurrying away one by one. His light exposed the tombstones in my heart that I had gingerly navigated around. His pure light beckoned me to open the lid on each tomb so that His light could fill up the shadows that were hidden there. The first tomb I opened was labeled, "Fear". Once it was opened and filled with the light of heaven, it disappeared and was replaced with a permanent imprint upon my heart that now says, "Jesus Was Here." I heard applause, then a cacophony of cheering permeate the coliseum. The legions of angels that filled this place were cheering for me...for me? Soaking it in, I felt a smile spread across my face as I looked back into the mirror and didn't recognize the woman who stood before me.

She carried a shield, held a sword and seemed a giant. I knew it was me because we shared the same face but the rest was unfamiliar. She was a warrior getting ready for a battle and she would fight, using the equipment handed to her by the mightiest warrior of all.

CHAPTER EIGHT

Standing Firm

Melodious, isn't it?
The message of Love
Raining down from our hearts

Often misting with
Tears of untold joy
Or sometimes drizzling
With melancholy voice

Drifting along
Through unbroken chains
Of years gone by

Lie haunting caverns
Hidden
In the dark and nether reaches

Yet somehow dawn
Approaches
And life begins anew
Without reproaches

Stretching our petaled arms
Towards the warmth
Of a fresh tomorrow

We,
You and I,
Can live on time
Neither begged nor borrowed
—Grant Johnson, Spring 1992

February 2007

The view from the top of the office building was breathtaking. The San Antonio skyline cut itself into the cushion of storm clouds that floated effortlessly between each building. The facades of each structure seemed to collapse beneath the weight of the clouds as each building disappeared inside the storm. *How appropriate,* I thought, that it would be stormy today. I looked around the office and decided to set my bags in the quilted armchair while I waited. I leaned my forehead against the plate glass and tried to see the bottom streets that stretched below. Waves of nausea rolled through my stomach as I stepped back and sank into the waiting arms of an overstuffed couch. *Come on girl, you've got to keep it together; there's no going back now.*

I focused my thoughts on all the reasons why I was there in that office, waiting to see what my future might hold. I focused on the previous months late night rantings, the Thanksgiving holiday Grant had missed, the torturous weeks between Christmas and

New Years that made me wonder if I needed medication, the Enchanted Rock debacle and then finally the trip to Robert's office that had finally shown me what I had to do. It was up to me to save my family and I had vowed to do whatever it took but never in all the years of loving Grant had I ever imagined I would be sitting in a lawyer's office.

"Mrs. Johnson," the lawyers' secretary came around the corner, "he's ready to see you now." She smiled encouragingly as I followed her around the corner. She opened the office door for me, and I silently nodded to her as I slipped through the entrance. I heard the door close with a click of its knob and found myself alone in what seemed to be a completely normal office. I fought the urge to call after her, hoping maybe she would stay and then realized how ridiculous that would be. I was there for a reason, was not backing out now and so I sat, clutching my quivering hands in my lap and waited.

My prayer had been to find a lawyer who would be an advocate for me. I needed someone who would be kind, and understanding, who might actually have compassion and not hang Grant out to dry. He was a family man, I could tell by the photos of his wife and kids on his desk, and perhaps even a believer as there was a cross hanging on the wall above his filing cabinet. When he walked in the door and I stood to shake his hand I was impressed by the gentle smile he shared and felt immediately at ease. He listened intently, took careful notes and nodded quietly as he wrote. He only interjected a few times as I told him our story and why I was there. I only wanted information about what my rights were, in case Grant were to die, or kill himself, where would that leave me? What if I needed to have him committed, then what? What if he left me, did I have a leg to stand on financially? I peppered him with questions that seemed endless; all the while he just smiled and politely answered each one. It felt like talking to someone who really understood my heart, he listened and that was how I knew I had come to the right place.

After what seemed to be hours, I was out of words and sat back in my chair. Only then did he say the words I never expected to hear from a divorce lawyer. He sat back in his chair, folded his hands in his lap and looked me square in the eye.

"Allison, do you really want to leave him? Because if you do I can certainly help you with that, but everything I hear you saying tells me that that's not what you really want."

I cleared my throat, "Well no, I don't want to leave him but you have heard all the reasons why I might have to, right? I came here to find out what my rights are. Isn't that what you do?" I felt confused by his comment. What did he think, that I had just decided on a whim to come and talk to someone about how to leave my husband? I felt frustrated and then before I had a chance to get angry. He smiled at me.

"Yes, I do understand why you are here, and believe me I've heard this kind of story many, many times. There are lots of different ways we can handle this but I want to encourage you to do something else first." He paused, and I could see he was ordering his thoughts carefully before he spoke.

"Allison, I never counsel people for divorce. You might be surprised by that since that's how I make my living, but it's horrible. You might think what you have gone through is the worst you could ever endure. I want to assure you, if you pursue this, you need to understand that it will be far worse than you could ever have imagined, especially with a person like your husband who is unbalanced and could be dangerous. I'm not saying that we don't have ways to handle that, what I am saying is this...I will help you and I understand your dilemma but I have also heard you say that you want to believe in your marriage, and in your husband. Before I ever begin divorce proceedings for a potential client I always encourage them to get counseling. In your case I want to encourage you to continue your counseling and know that you can call me anytime. If you decide that you need to pursue this, I will definitely help you, but I implore you to consider all the options before you do anything else." He handed me his card, shook my hand and then, "Allison, be very careful...trust your instincts, and know that God is with you."

It wouldn't be until later that day as I was getting ready for bed that I would realize how God met me there in the lawyer's office. He had answered my prayer by giving me someone who was indeed compassionate, and kind. He had also shown me that as much as I didn't want to pursue a divorce, there was a certain level of confidence I had gained by getting my questions answered. I was in the midst of a battle and the meeting I had with the lawyer was part of my equipping, if only in my mind.

I spent the rest of the day photo copying important papers, transferring money into my own account and packed emergency bags for myself and Zach and Kayla. I even picked a hotel in my mind that I knew was far enough away but not too far that would give me the ability to hide if I needed to. My parents were on notice to have their phones close by and one of my friends as well. I knew all of these things were part of my contingency plan that I hoped I wouldn't have to use. But I felt surer of myself, and enjoyed the knowledge I had gained. There was a fresh sense of peace in my heart that I believed had come from taking that step of faith. And how cool that God had delivered me to a lawyer who would end up being a Christian, which was certainly unexpected.

Don't get me wrong, I was not happy; in fact I felt such extreme guilt and sadness that I thought as soon as he returned from his trip he would know immediately that I had put an emergency plan in place. He was so good at figuring everything out, I was sure he would know what I was up to. So, I was far from happy with what I had done, in fact I was terrified, broken hearted and riddled with guilt. The worst part for me was wondering if the time came and I actually had to put my plan into motion, would I really be able to do it. Would I be able to get away? And if I did get away, would I want to stay away? The only way I could believe I was doing the right thing was to just keep asking God to show me, to remember the vision he had given me of washing away my stain and filth and how He had replaced it with the sword and shield I knew I now carried. I was in the throes of a battle so desperate and so life altering there was no way I could be sure of myself outside of the realm of trusting God moment by moment.

I used to think about women who left their husbands due to infidelity or physical abuse and think they were justified in their leaving. But I did judge them; thinking they should have found a way to work it out. How easy to judge something I knew nothing about, and if I could I would ask forgiveness from each person who had been on the receiving end of my judgmental attitude. How naïve to think that we can ever know what's really happening behind the closed doors of someone else's home, we only have our own frame of reference, and to judge someone from our limited knowledge is cruel and heartless. After everything Grant and I had been through I knew that I would never judge another person regarding their marriage, and would try to offer grace and understanding not unlike that which I had received from my friends and family.

Marriage is hard enough just because we all have our issues, we all have stuff. But when you add an ingredient like bipolar to the mix the outcome is never predictable and the end result is different every single time. It's not like a cake mix that comes out of the box, add an egg, water and some oil, pop it into the oven and you get a cake, every single time. Being married to someone who has bipolar is as unpredictable as anything ever was, and as painful as anything you could ever imagine and then some. It doesn't just happen to the person, who receives the diagnosis, it happens to everyone in the family, especially the spouse. And God forbid the children, those poor innocents who have no idea that their normal is constantly being upended by some invisible force, will only ever know this kind of normal.

If I was being brutally honest with you, I would tell you that even though I sensed God with me as I put my contingency plan into place, and I was so thankful for that, really I was, I would also have to acknowledge a very human response to what was happening. In one regard I felt empowered and surer of myself, independent even, which was fresh and exciting and fun. But I can't overlook the other extreme of emotions that played a huge part in my daily functioning: Anger. Breathtaking, exuberant, exhilarating, excruciating anger came with my empowerment, and I confess that it frightened me more than anything else. It felt good to be empowered and to have a fresh vision for how I could navigate things with Grant, but the anger singed the little focus I had, and overwhelmed me at every turn. I was angry about everything and anything. The littlest things set me off, the dishes in the sink, the laundry that needed to be folded, the dog needing to be fed, the dinner that needed to be fixed. Every single day I wanted to yell and scream and throw the biggest temper tantrum anyone had ever seen. I wanted to tell the world how I felt, scream it from the rooftops and shout to the heavens how much I hated my life, and how much I hated what God had allowed to happen to me and my husband. It crushed me with a vengeance and made me want to fold myself into a small box, close the lid and never come out. I just wanted to be angry, and so I was. Not in an overt way, but in more of an internal sort of way. I couldn't afford to express my anger to Grant, he was not in a place to handle it, so I tried to keep a lid on it to where it smoldered inside me, burning me up and you know that's just not a good thing.

To believe that I could have stayed that way for very long was really very naïve, but that's exactly what I thought. "Just put your plan in place," is what I told myself. "Just hang on and see what happens." Ha, that's ridiculous now when I think about it. The only thing that was constant in our situation was change that came daily. Nothing was predictable, nothing was easy and nothing made sense. Even though we tried to maintain normal activities there was going to be a breaking point and it was coming. Just like an arthritic knows a storm is brewing because their hip hurts, or a horse knows a tornado is about to strike, I knew somewhere in my unconscious mind that it was only a matter of time, something would happen to change where we were. I expected it, because I had learned to expect the unexpected. That's how it is when you're married to someone who has bipolar, you live on shifting sand, nothing is guaranteed, and nothing ever means what you think it means. There was no way that things were going to stay calm, not when there was a storm brewing inside me and he was getting worse instead of better. It was Plato that said, "No man ever steps in the same river twice, for it's not the same river and he's not the same man." We couldn't have gone back to do anything differently even if we wanted to. Too many variables were out of our control; too many factors were at work moving us towards this specific destiny.

July 3, 1993 Wedding Day

"Okay, Allison, let me adjust this back part of your train and I think you'll be good to go." The photographer tugged gently on the hem of my wedding dress, smoothing the wrinkles in preparation for the photos she was about to take. I smiled at the bouquet of pink roses I held in my hands and tried to breathe slowly. Today I was marrying the man of my dreams and I couldn't believe it. After so many long months spent apart we were finally going to be together. I couldn't wait to hear the pastor announce us as, "Mr. and Mrs. Grant Johnson." My heart swelled in anticipation as butterflies turned somersaults in my stomach. The photographer tugged one last time muttering to herself as she tiptoed carefully around the four foot train of my silk and lace wedding dress. I stood quietly smiling as she took photos of me. I couldn't stop dreaming of how Grant would look in his tuxedo as I had imagined for months what this day would bring. The photographer took a few steps farther down the aisle aiming the camera at me one last time. A grin consumed her face as her eyes met mine,

"Are you ready?" I nodded silently and then whispered, "Yes...yes I am." She turned and walked purposefully down the aisle that had been adorned with silk ribbons and pink roses. I watched her quietly open the door that led to the alcove where I knew he was waiting. The door closed behind her and for a moment I was alone in the sanctuary. Taking a deep breath I whispered quietly to myself, "It's okay, you're going to be fine, just don't cry when you see him." I closed my eyes imagining him in the black and white tuxedo we had picked out together. I knew his eyes would sparkle when he saw me and his smile would be for me and me alone. My heart sang in anticipation as it had for so many months. Our engagement had seemed an eternity even though it had only been six months since he proposed. The time had been challenging and there had been moments when I had really wondered if he would choose to marry me after all. My doubts were assuaged by the pre-marital counseling we had done and even that morning when he called me at the hair salon. "Good Morning Mrs. Johnson," his voice had poured over the phone line filling the room and my heart. "Good Morning to you Mr. Johnson," I had replied wishing I could hug him right then knowing it wouldn't be too much longer. I could hear the smile in his voice and then felt his love wrap itself around me as he ended our call with, "I love you Allison and I can't wait for you to be my wife." My heart sang with joy as I gently replaced the phone in its cradle. He chose me! He chose me!

I had never seen him look more handsome then he

did when he opened the door to the sanctuary. He smiled quietly as he strode purposefully down the aisle. I gasped at the sight of him, he was dazzling. My breath came in short spurts as I tried to take him in. He looked like a dream; the tuxedo fit his athletic build to perfection, the white tie a perfect contrast to his sun kissed cheeks. Oh how I love this man, I thought to myself as he practically ran down the aisle towards me. He took the stairs two at a time his blue green eyes sparkling with joy as he embraced me. Then as if he was looking at me for the first time he stepped back his hands holding me firmly at both elbows. He let his eyes wander over the full length of my body taking it all in. I could see him taking photographs in his mind as his eyes lingered over every aspect of my dress, every aspect of me. When his gaze landed on my face, a warm blush erupted across my chest and cheeks. He was looking at me with such tenderness and love, I felt it pierce my heart and I knew in that moment what it truly meant to love someone so completely and to be loved in return.

"Allison, you look so beautiful." I smiled back at him and quietly reached out to lay my hand against the slope of his neck allowing my fingers to glide up the plain of his cheek. Relaxing his face into the palm of my hand he closed his eyes as I whispered, "So do you my love, so do you."

CHAPTER NINE

Escaping

"Light and darkness, hope and despair, love and fear are never very far from each other." —Nouwen

And then I was running…as fast as I could…as far away as I could get. —Journal entry

Sunday, April 15, 2007

I wrapped the towel around my body and stepped carefully from the shower into the steam filled bathroom. It was going to be a rush but I was hoping we would make it to church on time. Grant was serving communion and I was looking forward to some good praise and worship time. It had been a challenging few days, we had argued Friday night, barely spoken to each other on Saturday and so far today it was too early to tell. Based on the quiet truce we seemed to have established I was cautiously optimistic that this day would be better and so I let hope bloom in my heart.

As I dug through my makeup kit searching for my under eye concealer I could hear him rustling around in the closet, probably trying to match his tie to his shirt, and let a smile play on my lips. That was something I enjoyed about his serving communion, he always wore his suit and looked amazing in it. I'll wear a pretty dress today too, I decided and maybe we'll feel like a couple again. I was determined to push aside the previous day's events, surely today could be a better day...please God, let today be a better day. I prayed silently to myself as I began applying concealer and then mascara. Grant had been so quiet on Saturday that I had given him a very wide berth. I knew that sometimes he needed space to process whatever emotions were flowing through his mind. On days like that I would carefully check in with him, "How are you," or "Is there anything you need?" He always said no, but it made me feel better to try and find a point of connection, especially when he was withdrawn. It was sort of like waiting for an alarm to go off that doesn't have a set time; you know it's going to blast at you only you never quite know when.

I decided to fix my hair after I chose a dress and wandered into the closet. He was standing in front of his wall unit choosing socks to match his shoes. He glanced at me and frowned as I moved to put my arms around him. "Honey," he said, "Can you help me pick out a tie?"

I smiled appreciating his request, feeling like this was a good sign, "Sure, of course," yes, I decided, definitely a good sign. I took a few steps closer to give him a hug when he dropped his shoes onto the floor. Something red sprawled across his stomach and caught my eye. I stopped arms in mid air and then quickly dropped them to my sides. I shook my head blinking to clear my sight, but when I opened my eyes again the red was still there, only this time I could see it was more than just a color, these were words and they screamed at me like demons straight from the pit of hell.

I stumbled then and grasped the wall for support struggling to keep myself from falling to my knees. Too stunned for words, I reached my fingers out to touch what used to be the smoothness of his skin. I wanted to believe it was as simple as picking up a sharpie marker coupled with intense boredom but knew as soon as my fingers touched the edges of the first letter this was way beyond something as simple as boredom and writing random words. I jerked my hand back as my skin burned from the words that blazed across his abdomen. Struggling for composure I gagged on the screams that were erupting inside me. Carved into the flesh of his stomach were the words, "FAT F***".

Tears burned at the corners of my eyes as I forced myself to look him in the eye, seeking to understand what would make him do such a thing. Internally I was screaming...Oh my God! Oh my God! Oh my God! Nothing had prepared me for this, and even though I was desperate for him to survive, I also knew in that moment that I wanted to be away from him. I wanted to run and run as fast as I could and get as far away from this sickness and this man who I no longer recognized.

"Oh, honey, what have you done? Grant what did

you do? What happened to you?" I searched his face for answers, hoping I would catch a glimpse of the Grant I knew and loved.

When he finally spoke it was in a voice that was defeated and heavy with sadness. His empty eyes pleaded with me as he searched my face wondering if I could understand the depth of his pain. He looked down at his stomach as if he had no idea what I was talking about and then I watched in horror as he gently stroked the words with his fingers, almost like he was energized by their presence. I knew in some ways he had relieved some of the internal pain he had been feeling, but it was so beyond my comprehension that even that little bit of knowledge didn't matter to me at all.

"Oh, this," he smiled cryptically, "Well, the feedback I've been getting from you and everyone else is that I needed to lose some weight. So I decided to give myself a little reminder. This is to remind me that I'm a fat f***. Now every time I look in the mirror I will remind myself that I'm not supposed to look this way. I'm not supposed to be this way." He walked away then, leaving me to gasp at the words that had forever been imprinted in my brain.

I couldn't look at him. I couldn't breathe, and the wails and screeches of hell echoed in my mind. We had fallen into the depths of hell where demons hovered all around us, waiting to strike, waiting to consume us with their claws and iron sharp teeth.

I mentally closed the door on the shrieks that were coming from my mind. It was incomprehensible.

Impossible to process and yet I couldn't escape the image of him standing before me with those ragged cuts embedded in his skin. Images of demons hovering over him as he took the razor and made the first cut danced through my head. I imagined him grimacing as the razor tore at his flesh, and then staring in wonder at the blood as it trickled into a pool onto the floor. If there had been any question in my mind that he was sick, it had been answered; this overwhelming knowledge came down like a crushing blow. I had walked right back into hell without even realizing it. Everything we had been working towards was lost in that moment. I forced myself to finish getting ready for church, numbing myself to the cries of despair that echoed in the empty chambers of what was left of my heart.

The problem was, I loved him. I knew it the first time we dated in high school. He made me want to be a better person, he made me a better person and I didn't know how to be that person without him. When he left me the first time I was terrified, my heart torn to shreds with nothing I recognized left. Empty, hollow sadness crept over me and through me every minute of every single day. I didn't know how to be without him, really couldn't be without him. I had given him my heart and I knew if he went away I would never get my heart back. I had loved him completely without holding back, and he made me believe it was real for him too. And then he did go away taking my heart with him, and I missed him desperately.

I missed him. I missed the him who I loved and

who had loved me in return. I missed his sweet eyes, his tender smile and his gentle loving ways. I missed all the times he made me laugh at his silly jokes and the way only he could make me laugh at myself. I missed smiling at him and getting a smile back. I missed hearing him say, "I love you." And I missed listening to him giggle and then erupt into a full blown belly laugh. I couldn't remember how long it had been since I had heard him laugh like that, or how long it had been since I had felt like laughing. All I wanted to do was lay down and cry, curling up into a little ball and never ever wake up. Instead I crawled into the truck with the kids and waited for him to get in the driver's seat.

I couldn't stop shaking. All through the ride to church, through the service and watching him serve communion, my body shook like an earthquake. I nodded and smiled and shook hands with friends, all while my body shook. Amazing what a person can do to keep things normal. It wouldn't be until later that afternoon, after I spoke with the doctor that the tears would come in place of the shaking, and when they came there would be nothing that would stop them.

"Mom," I dialed my parents as soon as I could. Throughout the entire service I had carefully calculated how I would navigate the afternoon and how I would leave if I needed to. It was time for me to put my plan into action. Grant had left to go running a few minutes after we returned home. "Well I guess I better go work on my pudge," he had said before kissing me on the cheek and walked out the door. I cringed inside as the door clicked behind him. It was hard to be in the same room with him, much less have him kiss me as if everything was just fine.

"Mom, you need to put Dad on the phone too." I said and wondered how they were going to react when I told them about the cutting. It was not unlike all the other secret phone calls I had made to them over the last months, only this time I wasn't crying and hiding in the bathroom imploring them to come and help me. This time I knew what I needed to do.

After a brief conversation with them and a "honey, you're going to be fine," comment from my Mom, I hung up the phone and immediately left a message with the doctor's answering service requesting they call me back as quickly as possible. I wasn't sure how to proceed but knew that once again Grant was dangerously close to needing immediate intervention. While I waited for the nurse to call me back I loaded Zach and Kayla's bags into the back of my car, grabbed my purse and threw a few things into a bag for myself. Somewhere in the back of my mind I knew it didn't matter to me what I took. Why did it matter what clothes I wore, or what makeup I had? Life as I knew it was about to change and I could have walked away with only the clothes on my back for all that it mattered.

I grabbed the phone on the first ring and waited for the automated voice prompt to finish before I spoke my name, "Allison Johnson for Dr. Peterson." The hum of the line echoed in my ears, filling the void of nothingness with what I imagined were bumble bees buzzing around. The nurse spoke first, "Mrs. Johnson this is Dr. Peterson's nurse, how can I help you today?" I sucked in a huge amount of air before I started speaking and then a torrent of words tumbled over themselves in a rush to make the most impact. She interrupted me briefly saying, "I need you to slow down, I can't understand you." I paused for a moment to catch my breath and then continued telling her about the cutting, the words imprinted forever in my mind and how afraid I was that he was going to harm himself and quite possibly very soon. "I need you to tell me what to do? I don't know what to do and I'm scared he's going to hurt himself, or go completely crazy and hurt me and the kids too. Please tell me what I need to do?" I gulped back tears that burned behind my eyes and waited for her instructions.

"Mrs. Johnson, I think I've told you this before; unless he calls us himself there isn't anything we can do. He's got to be the one to let us know that something is wrong. We can make a note of it, but unless he calls us and tells us he's in trouble there isn't anything we can do."

I interrupted her, "What do you mean? You and I both know that's not going to happen! How crazy is that? I mean, does he actually have to be suicidal before you'll step in?" I started to cry then, huge gasping sobs croaked out as I tried to listen to her ridiculous words. Was she serious? All this time I had thought that they would help me…now I didn't know what to do.

"Mrs. Johnson, the best thing you can do right now

is protect yourself and your children. If you have reason to believe that you are in danger then I think you need to leave. Do you have someplace to go?" Her voice reminded me vaguely of my kindergarten teacher when she was lecturing me about not tipping backwards in my chair.

"Well, yeah, but I'm not ready to give up. I mean…what if I call you when he gets back and he gets on the phone, would that work?" I knew I was negotiating with her but it was true, I wasn't ready to give up yet. I wanted to be sure that we were leaving nothing to chance. She agreed that would work so I hung up the phone grateful for the momentary reprieve we had negotiated. Now it was just a matter of getting him to tell them what he had done.

I called my friend Jaime and then Martha, putting them both on alert and then waited for him to come home. I laid my head down in my hands and begged God to intervene. *Please Lord*, I prayed, *please bring him home and make him willing to call and get help. Please Lord; don't make me do what I don't want to do. Help me know what you want for me to do and help me Lord to do it. I'm afraid God, I'm afraid, I'm afraid…*

As soon as he walked in the door I immediately dialed the doctor's direct line the nurse had given me to avoid the automated return call. She answered on the second ring, and I promptly handed the phone to Grant saying, "Dr. Peterson's nurse wants to talk with you."

He paused briefly, I could see the uncertainty in his eyes, but didn't try to explain. I knew the nurse would do that for me.

I listened to him answer her questions, telling her he was fine, there was nothing wrong and that he didn't have any idea why I had called. *Typical*, I thought, *they're going to think I've lost my mind and that I'm making up stories.* I moved to take the phone out of his hand and then thought better of it. Was I really expecting anything different? He had portrayed himself as just fine all along, I knew that was part of the compartmentalizing but I wasn't going to let it happen this time. I started to leave the room to get my notebook where I had been making notes of his erratic behavior when I heard something change in his voice.

"Um, I'm not sure what you mean," he said. I watched his face contort as he struggled to find the right words. Were they actually asking him about the cutting? He wiped sweat from his forehead and then the words I thought I would never hear came from his lips, "Well, yes I did cut myself...but I'm okay."

I could tell the nurse was pressing him since he nodded his head and grunted a few times before he finally told her that he had actually carved words into his stomach. "Yeah, I cut the words FAT F***, into my stomach but it's no big deal." He laughed nervously, and then said, "Ok, I guess I should come in."

He hung up the phone, glanced at me coldly and then left the room. I heard the water splash against the glass of the shower door tell me that he wasn't coming back. I sank onto the tile floor, relief and exhaustion rolling over me like waves crashing onto the beach. First relief, then exhaustion, relief, then exhaustion. I dialed my parents first, feeling relief that I wouldn't be leaving today; then dialed Martha and Jaime, feeling exhaustion that I wouldn't be leaving today. Then I curled up making myself as small as possible and rested my cheek on the cold, stone tile. *Thank you Lord, Thank you Lord. Thank you Lord.* I repeated it over and over again, until I couldn't form the words anymore. Then I buried my face in my hands and wept rivers of tears that didn't stop for days.

I had been fantasizing about leaving him off and on for a very long time. I imagined a little yellow house on the Oregon coast, working at a coffee shop while my kids went to a small town Christian school. I imagined a much simpler easier life and spent many days holding onto the yellow house as my safe place to which I would run if I had to. I fantasized about leaving him, not because I wanted to but because it felt like I had no other choice. It was obvious to me that my own safety and the safety of my children hung in the balance. How could I predict the volatility of our situation? How could I know whether his instability would turn on me and my children? There was no way to predict, and my maternal instinct kicked in. We had to leave. My children had seen and heard enough. I had no idea if they knew about his cutting, and hoped to God they didn't. But they had seen him sleep for entire weekends, punch holes in walls, drift aimlessly for hours on end and asked me repeatedly when I finished up a secret conversation with my parents, "Mommy why do you cry all the time?" We had to leave it was the only way we were going to escape the pit of hell that his illness had sucked us all into. We had to leave, it was the only way.

I made the decision after crying for two days, as I sat in Robert's office begging him to tell me what to do. After pleading and crying and wiping the snot from my chin with the back of my hand it clicked. We were leaving. I knew it like I knew in that moment there was nothing more I could do for him. Nothing I said or did ever made any difference. No amount of controlling, loving, supporting and encouraging could make any difference. I had known there really wasn't any "us" left and finally accepted there couldn't be any "us" until he got himself figured out.

"Robert, I think I'm leaving. No, I know I'm leaving and I'm taking Zach and Kayla with me." My voice echoed in the silence of his sun filled office. Yes, I was leaving, saying it out loud filled my body with adrenaline. I could feel the power of the words and the truth of them settling themselves into the deep wounds in my heart. I waited for him to respond, thinking he was going to try and talk me out of it. His response surprised me, although I'm not sure why, he above anyone else knew how hard I had been fighting to save Grant and our marriage.

He sat back in his chair, and said, "Great...when?" And then he smiled at me.

"Well, I'm not sure; I think I need to think it through. Zach and Kayla have a few more weeks of school. And I'm not sure what it would do to them if I just yanked them tomorrow." It had all seemed so simple just moments before, but I knew I had to consider them and the questions they would have and how would I explain to them that their Daddy had to stay here? I closed my eyes trying to clear my head. I could do this, just needed to get a few things answered. I knew I was going to Washington to be with my family but how would I get there and for how long would we stay? I began to process these questions out loud and by the end of the appointment had a pretty good idea of what was going to happen and where we were going and when.

Thursday April 19, 2007

We walked into Dr. Peterson's office together. He greeted us both with his customary handshake and smiled warmly at me. I couldn't help but wonder if he thought maybe I needed some treatment too. The last few days since Grant had talked to him had been a blur for me. The anxiety had been building in my heart ever since my appointment with Robert two days before. I knew I was going to tell Grant I was leaving while we had Dr. Peterson for an audience. I felt like a coward but also knew that he would not take the news well and I was afraid of how he would react.

I listened to their polite banter about the weather and golf and quietly nodded my head feigning interest.

Finally Dr. Peterson looked concerned as he said to Grant, "So, can you show me where you cut yourself?"

Grant laughed sheepishly while he pulled up his shirt, "Yeah, here it is." I watched Dr. Peterson carefully, looking for any change in his demeanor that would communicate to me how serious our situation really was. He sat back in his chair and said, "Do you think it's going to scar?"

Grant shook his head, "Nah, I don't think so; I've been putting stuff on it hoping to keep that from happening. I'm usually pretty good about that kind of thing." Yes, I thought, that's true which is why the fact that he had the cuts in the first place made me feel like screaming. I stared at Dr. Peterson willing him to get tough with Grant, willing him to ask him the hard questions about his behavior and how erratic it had been. I was prepared to fill him in myself but it would be so much easier if Grant would tell him the truth.

Dr. Peterson had always been careful in the things he communicated to us, and even now he didn't lose his measured tone or the thoughtful way he spoke. I could tell he was being very cautious with Grant; there was a rhythm to his questions. He moved in a little bit, then moved out, in and out. I wondered where he was heading and just as I was about to ask him directly he surprised me.

"Grant, I think we are dealing with something a little more complex than just a severe clinical depression. I think we need to get you off this drug and put you on something that is more of a mood stabilizer. I think we could very well be looking at a mood disorder called bipolar. The medicine we're going to move you to is actually used for people who have seizures but has been shown to be very effective with people who are dealing with a bipolar illness." He sat back in his chair letting his words sink in. He glanced at me and then spoke directly to Grant, "If you are not suffering from bipolar this drug will not do anything for you. If that is the case, we will have to continue trying some other things until we can get something that will work for you. But I am pretty sure this is the right direction. What do you think?"

What do we think? Was he kidding? I waited to see what Grant's response would be. This was the opportunity I had been waiting for; this was the time for me to agree wholeheartedly with Dr. Peterson...we had to try something new.

I heard Grant agree with Dr. Peterson that something needed to change. He looked over at me; I still had not uttered a word. His eyes were curious as they searched mine for understanding that I could not give. He smiled at me, squeezed my hand and said, "Ok, I'll try anything if it means that it will make things better. We've got to try anything if it means it will fix us."

The dam holding my tears broke with his last words. I tore my hands away from his and wept. I could not understand how in one moment he could be the loving, sweet husband I knew and then change before my eyes into the man who had caused us so much pain and suffering. I had heard all these things before, he would change, and things would be different. I had believed these promises before, only to have my hopes dashed time and time again. I could not at this point allow myself to be sucked back into the vicious cycle that his illness caused. I had to pull myself together, remembering there couldn't be any us, until he was better. In fact, there hadn't been any "us" for a very long time.

Clearing my throat, I wiped away my tears and avoided Grant's gaze instead speaking directly to Dr. Peterson. If I looked at Grant I knew I would fall apart again and I couldn't afford to lose the window of opportunity that had presented itself.

"Dr. Peterson, I can't do this anymore. I can't be here anymore...I have to go away for awhile." I could feel Grant's stare on my cheeks as they flushed with the heat that crept up from the burning in my heart. I felt his questions before he spoke them and knew I would have to answer them but first I had to say what I had needed to say for a very, very long time.

Dr. Peterson listened as I shared the burdens I had carried in my heart for so many months. I told of how Grant had wandered aimlessly for hours in Michaels and Wal-Mart. I told how he would disappear for hours at a time, only to reappear magically after leaving me to wonder if he would ever come back again. I told how he slept entire weekends away, and how when he woke up he looked like a zombie. I told about the endless nights where we didn't speak, how I had learned to diagnose his mood just by the way he looked at me. And finally I told how my children were asking me all the time now, "What's wrong with Dad," and "Why are you sad all the time."

Through my tears I finally looked at Grant, the burdens I had been carrying were no longer wrapped around my heart like a vise. Bewildered and confused he stared back at me, "But honey...what about us, are you leaving me for good?"

I shook my head ferociously, "No, no, no. This is not me leaving you for good!" Even though I really wasn't sure about that, I knew his survival hinged on whether he had any reason to live. I couldn't let him think I wasn't coming home. "No honey, I love you. This isn't me leaving you for good...I just need a break. I'm so exhausted, so tired of this roller coaster ride we have been on. I'm afraid of you and afraid for Zach and Kayla. I've got to get a break." He nodded at me quietly letting my words soak in. And then I spoke the words I had known to be truth for a very long time but never had the courage to speak, "Grant, there can't be any us, until you get yourself figured out. There hasn't been any "us" for a very long time." Blinking back tears, he sank into his chair as the last bit of life poured out of him. He was defeated and alone. I wished I could have taken back all of it, wrapped my arms around him and said, "Honey, it's going to be okay." But I couldn't, because I didn't know if it was going to be okay. And I didn't know if there would ever be any "us" ever again.

Dr. Peterson had been scribbling on his legal pad throughout the duration of my confession and the brief conversation Grant and I had just finished. Our eyes met and he smiled his kind smile that I had grown to enjoy.

"Allison, I completely understand. You need a break, you should go, and we will take very good care of him." And then, "You should know that anytime a person has been in a caregiver role it's not uncommon for them to reach burnout. I think this is what's happened with you." I nodded my head, yes burnout, I agreed wholeheartedly.

"Where will you go? When? And I think you should go for longer than two weeks. Once you've reached this level of burnout, you really need to have a long break. Otherwise, you could end up in the hospital yourself. I've seen that happen a time or two and that's not good for anyone."

Wow, he's agreeing with me, I thought. That was certainly not what I was expecting and I felt relief. I knew Grant would be well taken care of and there wasn't anything more I could do for him anyway. My leaving had nothing to do with wanting out of my marriage or not loving him anymore. I wanted my marriage to work and I loved my husband. My leaving had everything to do with caring for Zach and Kayla and getting the rest that I needed. I had no idea if anything would change with Grant on this new medication and treatment plan or if there would be anything for me to come back to. But I knew that as much as I had willed him to survive over the last two years, it was time for me to focus on my own survival trusting God to care for him now.

As I listened to Dr. Peterson discuss the new treatment plan, I felt a flicker of hope flash across my heart. It was time for me to get out of the way and let God do the work. It was time for me to put my trust in Him unconditionally, believing that whatever the outcome God had us all covered, He would care for us, provide for us and give us both the rest and peace that we needed. I had no idea what the future held for us, but I knew that God did and I was willing to trust him for it. I had to let go, it was time.

CHAPTER TEN

Defeat and Forgiveness

"They that wait on the Lord shall renew their strength; they shall mount up with wings as eagles; they shall run and not be weary; and they shall walk, and not faint." Isaiah 40:31

We left on May 10. It had taken exactly three excruciating weeks for the announcement I made in Dr. Peterson's office that I was leaving to become a reality. Walking out of the garage that morning I understood there was a very real possibility that if Grant didn't get better, that I could be coming home to an empty house. "Honey, what if he harms himself while you're away?" My mother had asked weeks earlier when I requested an extended stay at her house. At the time I couldn't acknowledge that I too, had been wondering the same thing and had been asking God to protect him. As I stood holding his hand in the airport security line I couldn't help but wonder if I would ever hold his hand again. Even though he was already taking the new drug the doctor had warned the side effects from coming off the other one could be severe. He was in a precarious spot and here I was leaving him to go and rest at my parents.

Conflicting emotions rolled through my mind as I smiled at him trying to soak him in, letting my eyes wander over the smoothness of his face. My brain struggled to memorize every aspect of him so that I would never forget the soft place next to his ear that I loved to rub, or the smoothness of his jaw as it flowed into the muscles of his neck. I let go of his hand so that I could place my arm around his waist, getting close enough to breathe him in. I buried my face in his neck breathing in the scent of his skin allowing my senses to be filled by his presence. He was my heart, my soul mate, my very best friend and I couldn't imagine living without him. With his arms wrapped around me, I felt my façade give way and ragged sobs ripped through my chest, shredding my heart and my will.

I loved him so much and yet I knew there was no way I could stay with him. I wanted to scream...NO, NO, NO. This couldn't be happening to us, it just couldn't. I wanted one last chance to fight, to save him, to show him how much I loved him. I didn't want to give up and I told myself that I wouldn't. That no matter how much time it took I would never stop fighting for the Grant I knew was buried deep inside him, the man I fell in love with who had loved me well for a very long time. I pulled my wet cheeks out of the safety of his neck and stared purposefully into his eyes. I had to see him one last time; I had to know that he was still in there somewhere. My eyes searched his, hoping for a glimpse of my sweet Grant, but instead I stared into dull lifeless eyes that had consumed any trace of life long ago.

He let his eyes connect with mine, and then looked away muttering, "I think it's time." Yes, he was right, it was time. I wiped my tear stained cheeks with the back of my hand taking a deep breath as I turned to Zach and Kayla. "Okay guys, it's time to say goodbye to Daddy." In turn they each wrapped their little arms around his neck covering his face with kisses as he squatted down to meet them eye to eye. To both of them he said, "I love you, and make sure you listen to your Mama." My stomach turned in knots as I took in the scene. Was I the only one who wondered if this would be the last time these precious innocents would see their daddy? I began to pray internally, asking God to help them memorize his face and his voice as I had done only moments before. And then finally it was my turn.

He took me in his arms again, wrapping his body around mine. I held him molding my body to his and then kissed him on the mouth drinking in the flavor of him I never wanted to forget. He whispered into my ear, "Honey, I love you. It's going to be okay, I'll see you in a few weeks." We had agreed that he would fly to Washington towards the middle of June to visit us and I was counting on him to make the trip. "I love you too." I said breathing deeply before I asked him the question that had been weighing heavily upon me for weeks. With my hands wrapped around the back of his neck, I kissed his cheek one last time and then whispered, "Okay?" His tired smile caught the shreds of my heart holding it warmly and then he quietly nodded his concession and whispered, "Yes, Okay."

I gathered my bags and corralled Zach and Kayla through the security line as he watched from the glass partition. He would wave and smile at the kids, blowing kisses back at them making them melt into giggles. I smiled at him over their heads, blowing my own kisses and internally asked God over and over again, to really make it be okay. We waved one last time before he turned and walked away. It took every part of my will to keep from crying out, "Wait, don't go!" But he was already gone.

I choked back my anguished tears and focused on getting the kids to the gate. Even though I knew we were doing the right thing, nothing had prepared me for the moment when I wouldn't be able to see him again. I cried out to God to hold us in his hands as he had been doing for so long. As the airplane lifted off, I asked him to give us the strength to deal with whatever came next and to protect Grant from the illness that was determined to destroy him. What I didn't realize was God had already begun the work. Even though I was afraid my leaving signaled the end of us, it was really just the beginning.

The withdrawal symptoms were more severe than Dr. Peterson had anticipated. For almost two years Grant's cocktail had been a mixture of an antidepressant, a thyroid drug, and a restless leg syndrome drug. The idea was to slowly take him off the antidepressant and the thyroid drug and at the same time increase the new drug. The balance was crucial, so crucial that Grant checked in with Dr. Peterson weekly in the early weeks while we were away. I found out months later he had endured intense brain shivers every time he turned his head too quickly. He felt sharp twinges of pain in his lower extremities, had headaches and cold sweats, coupled with hot sweats, nausea, vomiting, lethargy, insomnia, vertigo and continual thoughts of suicide. He grounded himself to our home, took some time off work, and wrestled with the invisible ogre that struck him at every turn. He insisted every time we talked that he was doing alright, even though he sounded worse to me, not better. I felt guilty for not being at home with him but at the same time knew I had nothing left to offer him. He was in God's hands and He was far more capable than I had ever been. He marked his time by focusing on the next Saturday that would signal he had survived another week and celebrate by spending the day with his parents, who were staying at a local RV park for the summer. God was really looking over Grant by sending his parents to be near him through that summer while I was away. They poured out their unconditional love to Grant and gave him hope to keep going.

Four years later, I have only just begun to understand the depth of energy and effort Grant poured into staying focused on his recovery. Not many bipolar patients stay on their medication, as well as endure significant withdrawal symptoms. The nature of the illness wreaks havoc on their ability to judge how they are really doing. Suffice it to say had Grant stopped his medication he would have ended his life.

True to his high achiever, driven personality he focused intently on his recovery. In spite of the horrendous side effects and withdrawal symptoms, he felt hope for the first time and clung to it with desperation. Like a man who floats lost at sea with only a life jacket keeping him afloat, this dim glimmer of hope became Grant's life preserver. While he missed having us with him, he was also relieved that he could focus all of his energy on doing only what he "had" to do, and knew that once he was better our relationship would be next on his list of restoration.

I arrived in Washington with Zach and Kayla hopelessly defeated. We spent the first few days in Seattle with my sister Holly acting like tourists and I somehow managed to keep myself together, at least on the outside. I slept a lot, drank a lot, and felt sorry for myself internally. My nerves were raw, and every little thing rattled me.

Moving away from the shambles of my life in San Antonio had broadened my perspective of how bad things really were. Grant and I had told the kids that he had to stay home to work, hoping they would believe us, doubting in our own hearts what the reality of our situation really was. In those early weeks of our separation I was sure I never wanted to go home. I didn't believe I could live with him if nothing changed with his illness. In the beginning, the emails and phone calls we exchanged were far from positive, filled with accusations and anger. The physical space between us gave some respite but there was need for emotional distance as well. I began to limit my contact with him, and didn't open many of the emails he sent me until I was in a stronger emotional place. It was just too painful.

Looking back, I wish that I had been a stronger more altruistic person but I know I wasn't. I wasn't brave or courageous or even very giving. At the time I didn't recognize who I had become and so of course had no idea how to love anyone except the bitter angry person who had taken me over. I longed for the place in my mind I recognized as the true representation of myself as a person and who we were as a couple. I remembered our friendship, our courtship and how much love we felt for one another and I fought to remind myself at every turn that the Grant I knew and loved was trapped inside his body. I hoped against hope that one day he would show himself again, I just didn't know how long I could wait.

After I had been in Washington for a few weeks the fog clouding my mind slowly started to lift. I imagined I felt like David must have felt when he wrote the twenty third Psalm. I loved this passage for the promises it made about God guiding us, providing for us, and being our complete and utter fulfillment. No longer was the girl in the mirror a stranger to me. She was someone I had ignored for a very long time and she desperately needed tending. I searched for my own green pastures and found them while surrounded by my parents, my sister in law, my friends through email, and my siblings. My still waters were found in the quiet walks I took in the morning and the silly games I played with the kids at night. My comfort came from talking with my parents and from writing in my journal. And of course I began to feel God's presence in a way that I thought I had lost; slowly the music in my heart began to reappear. Gladness replaced fear, joy took away my anger and peacefulness washed away my anxiety. The eyes of my heart slowly opened and I saw how we had indeed walked through the "valley of the shadow of death" and I knew "I would fear no evil."

I would love to be able to tell you there was one pivotal moment where I realized exactly what to do in order for us to live happily ever after. But, it wasn't like that. It was more like God reached his hand into my frozen chest and slowly warmed my heart, massaging it gently at first, coaxing it back into its familiar rhythm again. It had been such a long time since feelings like joy, happiness and hope had been a part of my vocabulary. I hadn't allowed myself to think about the future or even believe there might be a future. It felt good to be able to see myself again, hear the music in my heart and feel the familiar heartbeat that goes with me as a person. As days turned into weeks this familiar rhythm of who I am broke through the clouds of defeat and despair, showing me that I did have choices and chances and indeed a future life in front of me.

But in order to get there I had to get past myself first. I had to let go of the anger, the hurt, the pain and the feelings of failure and look defeat straight in the eye. I had to make peace with the fact that in this life there were always going to be things I would never understand. There were going to be memories that would cause me pain, which I hoped someday, would become shadowy fragments existing only in the periphery. If I was going to be with Grant I also had to accept Super Grant and Grant Zero as part of the package. And I accepted that I had no rights to anything really; I had no right to expect a happy ending or a peaceful life. These things were gifts, and to behave as if I was entitled was selfish and self centered. Ultimately I recognized it wasn't about me at all, but about Jesus and what he had done for me, and continued to do for me on a daily basis. Who was I to think that somehow where I was could possibly be his fault? Who was I to think that I was doing anyone any favors by being angry and bitter towards the very God who had saved me for all eternity? From the depths of my black hole of grief, I had finally reached the end of myself and I knew I needed God to reach into that pit and help me start climbing out. In my humanness, I saw defeat as failure and wore it like a crown of self worthlessness, but God saw my defeat as a chance to turn my eyes and my heart towards him.

Slowly I climbed out of my hole of grief, with the understanding that my feelings of defeat weren't the end of me, instead by facing them, I was given an opportunity for a new beginning. A new season of understanding was ushered in that brought with it a renewed sense of clarity...my old life was gone and that was hard to reconcile, but a new tomorrow was waiting. And as much as I wanted to fall in a heap on the floor and wallow in my defeat, that wasn't what God intended for me. He knew the true cry of my heart was to live, and there could be no living from the pit of grief, at least not the kind of living I wanted.

Grant didn't end up coming to visit us in June like we originally planned. In hindsight it was probably best that he didn't make the trip but at the time it was devastating to me. He sounded better at times and I would feel hopeful only to check in on him again a few days later and hear the angst and despair in his voice. He wasn't ready to travel. Even though his withdrawal symptoms were better, he was still struggling. I knew if we were going to go home it was time for me to make some hard decisions. Could I go home not knowing if he was going to get better? Could we be together again even though he was still in the midst of his recovery? Would I be able to maintain my new sense of focus and take care of myself? Could I forgive him?

I thought God would help me choose, and I tried to trust him to help me make the best decisions. There were moments when I was sure we were headed for divorce and I was moving to Washington with Zach and Kayla. And other moments where I knew beyond a shadow of doubt we were going home to Texas and going to do the best we could to make things work. I was still conflicted and my time was getting short. I had already changed our tickets once to stay a little bit longer. Zach and Kayla were starting to ask when we were going home and I didn't have an answer. It felt like our lives were hanging in the balance, what in the world were we to do?

In my own shortsightedness, I overlooked one of the greatest gifts I had been given and neglected to pass on to my husband. As much as I had discovered the truth about living in grief, embracing defeat and trusting in Him, had I learned anything about offering forgiveness and what that even looked like? I had long operated from the misconception that forgiving someone meant I had to approve of what they did. But forgiveness isn't related to approval and is in fact, more an act of unconditional love than anything my human brain could conceive of.

I had held onto the idea that somehow Grant was responsible for the terrible fallout his illness had caused and believed at some point that he would take responsibility for his actions while he was ill. The very idea that he would even begin to see the collateral damage that his bipolar had caused was naïve at best, especially given that he was literally fighting for his life. My lack of forgiveness was the final piece left in putting my broken heart back together again. It was time for me to acknowledge the hurt his illness had caused, accept it as part of the larger story of our life and let it go.

I asked God to help me see Grant through His Godly eyes. I asked him to change my vision, to open my eyes to the truth that was Grant's heart, the purity of his soul and the gentleness that was his spirit. I asked God to transform the way I saw him so that I could see him without condition or expectation. I asked God to help me get past myself so that I could see him through a clear filter and that was the beginning of me recognizing what true love and forgiveness were really all about.

Offering forgiveness isn't conditional; it's absolutely genuine, authentic and the purest form of love there is. Isn't that what Jesus did for us when He allowed himself to be placed upon the cross? He accepted the damage our sin caused and offered us the gift of unconditional love and forgiveness, allowing us to live a life in relationship with him. Offering forgiveness allows us to place the offender into the hands of the one who can deal justly with them and gives us an opportunity to look at our own sin and how we hope to be dealt with as well. Forgiveness isn't just a gift you give to others; it's also a gift you give to yourself. I chose to take myself off the path of unforgiveness, choosing to offer the gift of forgiveness to him. In the process I learned that offering this gift of unconditional love is worth far more to the person who gives it and to the person who receives it when there are no expectations attached.

And so I left Washington after two months knowing I never would have forgiven myself if I hadn't at least made an attempt to explore the possible restoration of our marriage. And I still loved him; I wasn't ready to throw that away. I came home because I had to try, one more time. I had to try for him and for Zach and Kayla and for me. I had to see if maybe it was possible to put our life back together again. I wanted to see if it was possible to exist together again beneath the same roof, navigating daily activities and family gatherings. I had to know if we could make it work with the new medications and the new attitudes and the different way we were. I had to know if maybe God indeed, had something more for us, maybe something good. Maybe we could actually be a family again, a modified form of who we had been, but a family nonetheless. I wanted that more than anything, I had to try. I chose to try.

But these aren't the only reasons why I came home. I wanted to see if maybe, just maybe we could reach through the shadows of our suffering and find each other again. I wanted to grab on to any part of him that I recognized and hold on as tight as I could believing that if I saw even a glimpse of the man I married, there was still hope and maybe, just maybe we could finally move out of the shadows of our suffering, into the light of God's love and begin the rest of our journey, together, taking it one moment at a time.

Walking Through a Miracle: Where We Are Today

"For we are God's masterpiece, He has created us anew in Christ Jesus, so that we can do the good things he planned for us long ago." Ephesians 2:8-10

How many of us would say that we would prefer to have a different life, or at the very least admit to ourselves that sometimes the path we are on is definitely not the path we would have chosen? And we feel angry about it, and we ask ourselves questions like, "What did I do to deserve this?" or "Why God, Why Me?" And we back ourselves into a corner that keeps us from being able to see more and we close our eyes to the obvious truths that are right in front of us...and we stay stuck believing that somehow our suffering is far more important than someone else's. And we reject anything and everything about the particular path we find ourselves on, hoping that somehow if we just pray hard enough that maybe God will deliver us from our little corner. We want to be delivered without having to struggle or suffer or fight or persevere. Remember that sense of entitlement I talked about before? That's what plunges us into deeper darkness when we see someone else delivered. And those old questions scream louder at us, and we wonder if God has forgotten us and why we can't be delivered too.

Being married to someone with bipolar does conjure up all these kinds of questions, especially when you see they are in the midst of a manic episode, or in the throes of a deep depression. Watching and waiting to see if the person you love is going to come around again is one of the worst parts of dealing with mental illness and I used to beg God to deliver us from it, every single day. But I don't anymore, partly because we have been lucky and Grant is doing very well on his medication. In fact he is really a model patient. This is not a simple fact to be overlooked, given how statistics show that most bipolar patients are almost guaranteed to stop taking their medication at some point during their treatment. But even if Grant wasn't doing well, and don't think for a minute that I don't wonder sometimes if we are living on borrowed time, I still wouldn't ask God to deliver us from it. No, I don't ask God to deliver us from it anymore and it's not because I enjoy having this illness be a part of our lives. I stopped asking God to deliver us from it when I started to see the little bits of life that bloomed because of it. And I probably stopped asking God to deliver us from it because really, that way of thinking is an energy drain for me and doesn't allow God to really take hold and do the work He wants to do. Whether we like it or not, this illness is a part of our story and part of the way that God makes himself known to us every single day. Sometimes we are mad and we let him know it, other times we are sad and we let him know that too. Would we much rather have God make himself known to us through something a lot more joyful, of course! But we've come to a place of acceptance where we know that this is God's will and his plan for us. We try every day to accept it and most days in spite of our humanness; manage to be thankful for it.

People ask me all the time, "Where are you today?" and "Do you ever stop worrying about whether he'll get sick again?" These are questions I ask myself all the time, and sometimes I know the answers and sometimes I don't. Most days I look at Grant and see the man I married who is alive again because of his medication. I see the new and improved version and I really like him...a lot. He makes me smile and laugh and knows my heart inside and out. He makes my heart sing with joy when he touches me in just the right way and his voice soothes me in the night again when I'm afraid, just like he used to a long time ago. I know we are extremely fortunate to be in this place, and to have his illness very well controlled. That doesn't mean he doesn't have bad days like everyone else. It's those days I feel that catch in my spirit when I see the yellow flags pop up that may indicate a depressive cycle or a potential manic episode. Even with medication he still cycles, just not nearly as bad as he did before. We also know from experience that he does better when there isn't too much on the agenda and when we are together as a family, functioning in our routine. I think of the bipolar as being in remission. It will never truly go away and because of that will always be a part of him and a part of me as well. Now I know that the best thing is to be here, in this present, letting the things of the past fade away and I try very hard to not worry about the future.

When I came home from Washington we didn't have naïve expectations about where we were. We could see the long and arduous road laid out before us if we wanted to save our relationship. Those first few weeks were hard. My conditioned response was to always be on my guard and I had to really lean into God trusting him to hold me close as I slowly let my guard down. Eventually I stopped looking over my shoulder wondering if when he came home what kind of mood he would be in. Slowly I began to see little signs of life bloom where only death and despair had lived before, and I felt like I could breathe again. The simple things like him driving the carpool to soccer, or helping clean up the dinner dishes, or watching SpongeBob with Zach and Kayla gave me hope that maybe he was getting better. But the most telling indication was the way he was. He was gentle and kind, thoughtful and sweet, silly and playful...all things he had been before, only more so. I was so astonished by the transformation that I would stare at him when he didn't know it because it amazed me to see the light in his eyes again and the smile on his face.

When I came home from Washington, I had my own list of tolerations and non tolerations that I wouldn't compromise and I still don't compromise them now two years later. He has to take his medication, he has to go to the doctor and if any kind of violent behavior takes him over again...well, then I have to leave with Zach and Kayla. I know that sounds harsh but it's so important to know how to navigate this illness and keep yourself safe at the same time. My time in Washington taught me that it was okay for me to listen to my own heart, set my own safety boundaries and trust God to give me the strength to flee if I needed to.

Do I still worry about him getting sick again? No, not really, but I do pay attention to what goes on in his daily life that I know can signal a cycle into depression or mania. I don't babysit him or remind him to take his medication, but I do make sure he has his prescriptions filled on time and will periodically check in with him about when his next doctor's appointment is. We've managed to figure out what works for us. Any marriage needs good communication and we are certainly no different; we just have an added ingredient.

Grant is alive today because God worked a miracle in his life. The outcome could have been radically different and we know we are extremely fortunate to be in this place of healing and restoration. We also know there are approximately six million people (2.5 percent of the population) in the United States today who have been diagnosed or will be diagnosed with bipolar. Their paths will be unique, the only common thread being their diagnosis. Nothing about this illness is predictable and many of these people will lose their lives because of it. Others will be fortunate, like Grant, to have found the right medication and will be able to maintain their treatment regimen. For those of us friends and family members, our lives will never be the same as we fight right alongside them on a path we would not have chosen but find ourselves on nonetheless.

When we were in the worst part of the storm we both existed in our own private hell. Mine was grief, Grant's was pure horror. We needed to see the end, and because we couldn't at times we felt abandoned and alone. We both wanted to be able to count the days until this horrible sadness would be over. We wanted to know when everything would feel right again and kept asking God...When will this be over? When will our life be better? We were desperate for answers so that we could put our hope in something, believing anything would be better than where we were.

As we moved farther into Grant's healing process and our relationship began to improve I wanted to know if anything good would come from our struggles. Certainly I could see how our family was being restored but I wondered if maybe God had something more for us, and was it something we could pass on. I guess I wanted to find a reason for our suffering. I had heard stories of people who had gone through tremendous suffering and had admired them and their fortitude in persevering through their challenges. But I hadn't imagined that God would choose to use our challenges with bipolar as encouragement to others. Was that his purpose for us? To use what we had gone through to support and encourage others who had walked a similar path. 2 Corinthians 1:3-5 refers to God as being "the father of compassion" and the "God of all comfort." He comforts us in all our troubles so that we can pass comfort on to others. In this way our suffering becomes one of our most precious assets. Now when I meet someone, I wonder what's happened in their life, what their story might be and what kind of comfort they might need down the road. That's part of the purpose behind our suffering. We understand now that we are called to comfort others, passing on the things we learned through our healing. Not for our own selfish gain but to further the kingdom of God, serving others out of the unconditional love that we have received.

It's been a painful process and one we would not have chosen but we acknowledge that this is where we have been and this is who we are now, because of this season in our lives. Perhaps bipolar will always be a part of us, but we know that God is big enough to handle it and while we may not know what tomorrow will bring…we know that God does and so we trust him for it, believing that when and if the bottom falls out again, he will catch us and care for us and lift us up.

It could have been so different for us. Grant could have died that day, leaving me behind to grapple with an illness that I really knew nothing about. But instead God intervened, and carried us through the most horrific storm we could ever have imagined. To try and sum it all up in one final chapter feels almost impossible...the story isn't finished yet so we won't say "The End". Instead we will say, "The Beginning", because that's exactly where we find ourselves today—at the beginning of something new, something that is bright and alive and filled with hope. We're at the cusp of a new chance at love and we want to embrace it fully, living here in this moment knowing that tomorrow is in God's hands, trusting that He will provide and meet us right here right now. I call it our Resurrected Life—the gift of healing and restoration like when Jesus raised Lazarus from the dead. How long will it last? We don't know. Will there be a time when we have to adjust medication or endure another difficult season? Most likely...yes. But there are no guarantees for any of us regardless of our relationship status or physical and emotional state. There are no guarantees in this world that I know of except for one. As children of God we are guaranteed life in Christ, here on this earth and then again when we die and go to heaven.

We can't deny the deepening of our faith and the way God's hand of protection wrapped around us providing us a place of refuge in the midst of the storm. We don't know why God chose to deliver us through the fire, that's a question I would like to ask

God when I get to heaven. In the mean time Grant and I are choosing to live for this point in time, focusing on rebuilding our marriage and raising our kids. We accept this gift of Resurrected Life knowing that it might not last forever...and we're okay with that. The Bible says that God doesn't give us more than we can handle so when the next storm comes, we will try and remember what we have learned and hopefully we'll remember that trusting God is so much easier than trying to handle things on our own. He's certainly big enough to carry it all, so we're going to let him.

RECOMMENDED RESOURCES

Associations and Organizations

The National Institute of Mental Health

The Depression and Bipolar Support Alliance

The National Alliance on Mental Illness

Overcomers Outreach

Family Life Conference

Celebrate Recovery

Suggested Reading

Bipolar Disorder: A Guide for Patients and Families, by Francis Mark, M.D., Johns Hopkins University Press (1999).

A comprehensive guide for patients and families, this is a book that emphasizes advantages and disadvantages specific to treatment options, support systems and emergency planning.

The Bipolar Disorder Survival Guide: What You and Your Family Need to Know, by David J. Miklowitz, Guilford

Press (January, 2002).

This book is intended for patients. It spends a good deal of time on issues exclusive to the sufferer, how to come to terms with the diagnosis, whom to confide in, and how to recognize one's own mood swings.

Loving Someone with Bipolar Disorder, by Julie Fast and John Preston, New Harbinger Publications (February, 2004).

This book is written for the partner of someone with bipolar mood disorder. The format is easy to read and intended to provide the partner with tools to help work through the challenges of living with someone with this mental illness.

When Someone You Love Has a Mental Illness by Rebecca Woolis, Penguin (November, 2003).

This book is written for someone who loves or cares for a mentally ill friend or family member. It covers the basics of mental illness in a handbook format offering crucial advice and guidance.

The Burden of Sympathy: How Families Cope With Mental Illness, by David Karp, Oxford University Press (May, 2001).

This book is intended to be a helpful cohort for those seeking guidance through the many issues that arise in dealing with mental illness. By sharing stories of families across the world, Burden of Sympathy provides a companion resource for those in similar situations.

An Unquiet Mind, by Kay Redfield Jamison, Vintage (January, 1997).

Told from a survivor and healer's perspective, An Unquiet Mind offers insight into the tremendous challenge presented in living with bipolar mood disorder. This is an insightful memoir of one person's life and how it has been colored by bipolar mood disorder.

Boundaries in Marriage, by Dr. Henry Cloud and Dr. John Townsend, Zondervan (August, 2002).

This book, like all those in the Townsend/Cloud series, is very specific in offering guidance to healthy ways of relating. It helps define who is responsible for what behavior and how to handle those that are out of control, whether it is your spouse's or your own.

Love Must Be Tough, by Dr. James Dobson, Tyndale House Publishers (April, 2007).

This book focuses on tough love principles applied to marriages in crisis with a strong, direct approach while offering guidance through difficulties such as divorce, separation, infidelity, or abuse.

The Marriage You've Always Wanted, by Gary Chapman, Moody Publishers (July, 2005).

This book is focused on the challenges often met by couples in marriage. It is meant to confront individuals in their own behavior and shift the focus from what their spouse is doing to look at themselves and seek their own personal transformation.

Breinigsville, PA USA
06 January 2011
252834BV00001B/58/P